EDITED BY JAMIE FOSTER BROWN

A Sisterfriends' Tribute in
Words and Pictures

Betty Shabazz.

↙ TITLE ENTRY

SIMON & SCHUSTER

v1. SHABAZZ, BETTY
v2. BLACK MUSLIMS- BIOGRAPHY

SIMON & SCHUSTER
Rockefeller Center
1230 Avenue of the Americas
New York, NY 10020

SIMON & SCHUSTER *and colophon are registered trademarks*
of Simon & Schuster Inc.

Designed by Karolina Harris

Manufactured in the United States of America

10   9   8   7   6   5   4   3   2   1

Library of Congress Cataloging-in-Publication Data
is available.

ISBN 0-684-85294-2

I want to beat up my friend Von Alexander and my agent, Eileen Cope, for getting me into this.

Special thanks to Northern High School librarians Shirley Britton and Evarnie Mouzon, my cousin Janet McElrath, my editor, Bob Mecoy, Bob's assistant, Pete Fornatale, and my administrative assistant, Evonne Jackson.

Special thanks to Dr. C. DeLores Tucker for her insight and for helping to steer me to one of Betty Shabazz's best friends, Laura Ross Brown.

And more special thanks to my husband, Lorenzo, who thought I had lost my mind when I took on this book with all of my other responsibilities. But, as usual, he saw me through it. Love ya, baby!

Also, special thanks to my good friend Anna Perez (and again Lorenzo) who pulled me through in the final hours of deadline.

JAMIE FOSTER BROWN

To my mom (Nee), thanks for the love; and to Dr. Jimmy Jenkins, Sr., thank you for the time off from Edward Waters College.

VON ALEXANDER

For my gramsie and granddaddy,
Estella Mae and Flemma Harris, Sr.;
my mother and father, Mamie Lee and Peter J. Foster;
my sisters, Estella M. Foster and Shirley Hunter;
my late brother, Warren Foster;
my aunts, Essie Foster, Ruthie Mae Williams, and Berniece Gorham;
my uncles, John Harris, Sr., and the late Flemma Harris, Jr.;
and my sons, Russell and Randall.

Contents

Preface

ON MARCH 13, I dreamed about Dr. Betty. A soft, easy dream. We were riding on a bus. I was standing up leaning on the back of a seat. So was she. I turned and said to her, "You know, Betty, I've written a book about you and it's coming out this summer." She turned and with the same smile she has on the cover of this book, she said, "I just love the way *we's* get busy when we've got the Lord's work to do." This dream was my first and only conversation with Dr. Betty. Still, this book was a labor of love and good stuff.

For years, I loved Malcolm X's voice, his mind. When I was a child, my father would tell us to sit down and listen to recordings of Malcolm's speeches. My father would say, "See, he's so quick, he answers folks' questions before they can even ask them. He knows what they're going to say before they even say it." He loved him some Malcolm X and my father didn't love many folks in those days.

Malcolm's beautiful wife, Betty, was always an enigma to me. I admired her. I was in awe of her. And for those reasons, I never got close to her. I remember being amazed to learn that after Malcolm's assassination, she managed to raise six daughters on her own, get a Ph.D., teach at Medgar Evers College, and that she'd done all this and still managed to travel constantly—speaking, helping, teaching, counseling, and furthering her husband's name and work.

I often saw Betty at parties and events, but there were always tons of folks around wanting to meet her. She was like a rock star. Even if I'd had the nerve to try to talk with her there, it just never seemed possible. Still, every time she saw me, she would give me a hug and hold out her cheek for me to kiss.

After I learned that Dr. Betty had been severely burned, I asked one of her closest girlfriends, Dr. C. DeLores Tucker, what Dr. Betty was really like. Dr. Tucker began telling me about the less serious, very fun side of Betty, and how generous and loyal she was to her girlfriends.

During those painful days after she was hurt, the world finally noticed what a treasure was being taken away. Everyone realized all that she — and Malcolm — had done for us all. At the funeral, many people made speeches about Betty's accomplishments, but the most wonderful stories were those that her friends shared — their memories of and experiences with Dr. Betty. These were little vignettes that revealed the shopper, the gourmet cook, the dancer that was also Betty Shabazz.

I started interviewing more of Dr. Betty's friends, hoping to capture some of these stories for my magazine, *Sister 2 Sister*. Von Alexander, who helped me put this book together, was the one who suggested that I talk to *lots* of Dr. Betty's sisterfriends and get them to help me make a book and do something for Dr. Betty's daughters. You're not going to find a lot of speeches and fanfare here. You're going to learn the rest of the story.

For example I always wondered where Betty went, who harbored her and her children after Malcolm's murder. Ossie Davis told me it was his wife Ruby Dee's brother and sister-in-law, Thomas and Antoinette Wallace. Betty was already living with them after her home had been firebombed just a few weeks earlier. Attallah Shabazz told me Brother Thomas was later stalked and beaten. He's since passed on. God bless him and Sister Antoinette.

I am honored and tickled pink to be the one to pull all this together, to discover who were her sheros, what she was like in high school, even who did her hair. And I think that you'll be happy to see just how wonderful, full, exciting, and intriguing a life she had.

This is not a full biography of Dr. Betty Shabazz. We leave that up to her family and to historians. What you'll find here are personal essays from some of her sisterfriends—an attempt to capture on paper the way people felt about her and saw her when she wasn't being *Dr. Betty Shabazz,* but Betty Sanders, the little girl still inside Dr. Betty Shabazz.

First Word

MYRLIE EVERS-WILLIAMS *is chair emerita of the National Association for the Advancement of Colored People (NAACP). She is the widow of slain civil rights leader Medgar Evers and director of the Medgar Evers Institute. Her book,* Watch Me Fly, *will be published in the fall of 1998.*

I saw an ad on television. It asked who the most important person of the year was; what the story of the year was. Maybe it was a magazine ad. A bunch of faces flashed by, and I saw Betty's face. I felt such pain, because my friend was gone, but I felt anger, too, because she was a woman who, until her death, the public didn't appreciate. And I guess I found myself asking why people have to die before we recognize the full-blown beauty, the strength, and the generosity that they possess. I know that that's the norm because of all that we have in this world, all that's facing us, all that's bombarding us from television and other media. Most of this is very insignificant in the whole scheme of things, but Betty wasn't. She made a certain impact on a lot of lives, without a lot of fanfare. And she was so much more than Malcolm's widow.

That we were more than just "widows of" was one of the threads that connected Coretta Scott King, Betty, and me, and it was something that the three of us—particularly Betty and I—talked about. Betty was fun— she was *so* funny. Betty loved to dance—she *loved* to dance. I used to love to dance, and I still enjoy it, but thinking about it, we would often reminisce about our earlier lives. Dancing with our husbands, being so close. How our hearts would beat in anticipation. Betty would describe the movements and everything. Betty was fun.

I recall the first time that Betty, Coretta, and I went on a retreat. The day Betty was burned came just a few days before we were to go off together again. We had been together since that first time, but this was going to be the first time since then that we would get away. Just the three of us without any folks listening. Without any witnesses. Just as girlfriends.

I think that that first trip was Coretta's idea that we just get together and relax because we were all under such tremendous pressure. It seemed like there was nowhere we could let down and be ourselves. I got there a day before they did, and when I saw them for the first time, they had just checked in and had come over to the area where the exercise wing and sauna was. When they saw me, Betty said, "Girl, what happened to you?" I don't know how I looked, but I must have looked as though I was inebriated, because I was certainly walking like I was inebriated. And I remember her saying that if it quacks like a duck, it must be a duck.

I could barely stand; I was weaving. I was intoxicated from a massage, which had me so weak, I was all but floating. Betty was shocked because she had never seen me look like that. She got this silly smile on her face, and while Coretta was still looking at me funny, she said, "Girlfriend, I want some of that." It was that kind of thing because we had never really been able to get together without the façade of our being "widows of" or what not. All during our stay, Betty and I went without makeup. Without anything — I mean, just in our grungies. My hair, I just washed it and let it go. There was no styling. No makeup, no nothing, just free. We teased Coretta because she made herself up so beautifully every day and went to sit by the pool.

That was the first time we had reached out to each other this way. I had invited both Betty and Coretta to visit me at my home in Oregon, but everybody's schedule is busy. They teased me about living in the country so far removed from everything, and I'd tell them they didn't know what they were missing — around here we have nothing but peace and quiet. And then I would challenge them by asking them if they could deal with the quiet, because we were running so hard that we didn't know we could have any other life.

When we were together, we talked about almost everything. We had made a pact not to talk about our jealousies, but just to be girlfriends. (I keep using that word.) Just being girlfriends, as we'd say, just to hang. At the spa, we went to this dance exercise class, and it was only the three of us in there. Betty and I tried to get Coretta to join us but she said, "Oh, no." She was very, very sweet and she laughed and carried on about it. So when the instructor put the music on, Betty started moving and said, "Come on here. Myrlie, come on."

We got up and were doing the electric slide, and Betty was carrying on like crazy. She said to the instructor, "We need to do something else. I know how to do the electric slide and she's doing okay. What else you got?"

The young woman started teaching us the Achy Breaky. Betty picked it up right away, and I accused her of already knowing all the dances and just trying to show me up. I never did get it down, but she had it.

She was such a quick study because she loved it. She loved it and she would laugh and tell you to come on, you can do it too. She just had this free spirit, in the best sense of the word. When she laughed, she had this beauty; when she smiled, it lit up the whole room. She could laugh and make you come out of yourself enough to chase away whatever might be weighing you down; she just had the ability to lift you out of it. That was just kind of magical.

One day, while we were at the spa, the three of us were in Coretta's suite, and there was a basketball game on television. The shock of my life was seeing not only how into it Betty was but how much Coretta enjoyed it, too — in the same way that Betty had me dancing, she had Coretta hooked on basketball. We were seeing sides of each other because Betty had the spirit that could make you let go.

♋

O U R relationship didn't start at that spa. We had been talking for years. Being in each others' company, talking, and chatting on the phone. We talked about our marriages and how we both blocked out — I don't want to call them problems — *challenges* that would be difficult in any marriage. One thing in particular that Betty told me about Malcolm was that she'd get angry with him. She said, yeah, she'd get angry, and she'd go home to her parents' house — and every time she came back to Malcolm, she got pregnant. I won't go into details about that, but Betty could be pretty graphic.

There was such love in that relationship. Betty did not tell me the deeply intimate things that she and Malcolm shared — only a couple of moments — but that was enough for me to know, because of my own experience with Medgar, that there was a lot of love there. Malcolm was a loving man. Betty never had to question whether or not he loved her —she knew. He was gentle, he was kind, he was a good father and a wonderful friend.

ℬ

BETTY seemed never to be jealous or resentful of anyone's happiness. She was always there to help. It was interesting to me, for example, that she was teaching at Medgar Evers College, at an institution named for another civil rights leader, one who certainly was not as recognizable as Malcolm. She was there to do a job, to help the students there and to lift the college. And that, in itself, shows how big she was. She was the one who thought to change the name of the street that the school was on to Medgar Evers Lane. You know, just big of spirit, big of heart.

ℬ

I remember saying that at least Coretta was spared. She and her children were spared seeing her husband and their father shot down. But when we approached that area, Betty would kind of grab on to me, and we knew each other, and knew each other's pain, well enough that we also knew enough not to push each other into talking about it. We all knew the pain, and when it got bad we could hold hands or embrace. It wasn't necessary to say anything. We knew.

Oh, my God, the way Betty died. I was devastated. I could not believe it. I kept praying that the burns were not that bad, that it was not that severe. And then I did something that is unusual for me these days; I started asking why. Over the years, I've reached a point in my faith, where I believe that all things have a purpose. But now, I kept asking why. Why Betty? She didn't deserve to be hurt like that. She was a woman who I had known to do nothing but try to help other people. Her goodness, her light, the joy of being around her, and then having that happen to her.

Finally, though, when I knew just how severe her burns were, I said, "Lord, go on and take her. My daughter said to me, "Mom, that's the wrong prayer." I said, "I don't want her to suffer. I don't want her to suffer."

I went to the hospital. My heart was breaking, but I had to talk to her. I had to talk to her in the same way that we had always talked. I walked out of that room not knowing whether a miracle would take place, and I still to this day do not know why this happened, except I look at all the beauty that she has left behind. I went back to the hospital knowing that more than likely I wouldn't be able to see her again, but I knew how much her daughters meant to her, and I wanted to be there for them. I just wanted to be there to embrace them, to love them because they were extensions of Betty and Malcolm.

Betty and I had talked about our own demises in a kind of a casual way, and we both agreed that we didn't want to be burdens to anybody. We hoped that when our time came, it would be quick. I remember that.

Since Betty died, Coretta and I have just talked back and forth. She's consoled me and I've consoled her, but I'm one of these folks that cry at the drop of the hat. The tears came that first day and later as I asked, Why, why, why? There has to be a reason for her lingering like this. And I prayed to God that maybe she would be one of those miracles that come through and survive with so much wisdom and strength and peace and love to share with us that she'll guide us. Like everyone else, I was searching for something good in this.

One thing that did happen was that the American public realized what a magnificent human being Betty was. Perhaps if she had died in her sleep, her death would not have had the same impact. There are young women who knew that Malcolm left a wife, a widow with children. But now they get to know her intimately through her strength, through her holding on. I believe Betty held on for as long as she did for a reason. I knew when I got home and I stood on the deck looking at the mountains, my favorite place. The sound of the wind blowing, the peace, the quiet, the serenity. I was able to say, "Go, sister, go." It was like I was setting her free in my heart. I was finally at a point where I could say, "Betty, you deserve the freedom and the peace, and the love and the joy that I know you've experienced because your spirit is free." I love life and so did Betty.

Introduction

VON ALEXANDER *became at the age of twenty-one the first African-American woman to trade over-the-counter stocks. She has spent more than eighteen years working as a media specialist in the entertainment industry, where she has worked with Nelson George, Melba Moore, and Dionne Warwick, among others. She is also the director of the National Political Congress of Black Women's entertainment commission, as well as assistant to the president of Edward Waters College in Public Relations. She lives in Jacksonville, Florida.*

WAITING for Betty's memorial service to start, I watched excitedly as the majestic expanse of Riverside Church filled up with just about everybody I could ever think of admiring. I was supposed to have come with Dr. C. DeLores Tucker, but she had to travel with the Shabazz family, and so she told me to tell everyone that I was her guest. I did, and, sure enough, all my sisterfriends were there, large and in charge. When I arrived, I saw my girlfriends Toni Fay and Caroline Jones. We made our way back to the VIP holding room, kissing and hugging, very glad to see everyone, trying to keep from crying while admiring the fact that we were all there. I had never ached so much. Amy Billingsly, Barbara Skinner, Hazel Dukes, Jean Owensby, and all the other brothers and sisters did an outstanding job. Sister Betty would have been proud.

To be there and have known her was an honor, but I had to laugh a little. I said a quiet prayer and then told Dr. Betty, "Girlfriend, it took your death to get all these divas together in one room. Any other time you couldn't get them all together." It was like she summoned them and said to all, It's your last time to show me love, or I will come back to haunt you. I suspect that she would not have said it so nicely, though.

As I sat there waiting for the service to start I thought about our special private lunch two weeks before her accident. Dr. Tucker (may God always continue to bless her) had arranged this meeting by asking me to talk to Dr. Betty about some shopping problem, even though I told her that I didn't know Dr. Betty like that. Dr. Betty was one of my sheroes and mentors, and I respectfully admired and feared her. So when she called me to say that she wanted me to call the St. John's Knits show-room and tell them that she wanted to shop, that she wanted a better deal on her clothing, and that she didn't have time to shop during regular hours, I called Dr. Tucker. Didn't this woman know she was really black and that these people didn't care who she was, let alone how much money she was spending, unless she's bringing the pope? Dr. Tucker told me to call the showroom and do as Dr. Betty said, "because you did it for me. Don't forget you are our miracle worker. Well, I called, and they laughed at me and said that they were already giving her a very good discount, and that every few months she put someone else up to calling and trying to get her a little better deal. I felt so stupid, but what was going on was that these women were playing healing games with me. (One thing you must keep in mind — these women knew how to love and heal you without you even knowing it.)

I called Dr. Betty back and said I had the information for her. She replied by asking me to pick any place I wanted to go for lunch. I chose Il Tinello, a wonderful restaurant in New York City on Fifty-sixth Street where the owners, Mario and Francesca Fabris, always made me feel special whether I had money or not. My safe haven. Il Tinello also became the place where Dr. Betty fell in love with the Grissini breadsticks —she loved them so much she wanted to buy some, but, of course, Mario, being the wonderful host that he is, gave her a shopping bag full for free. He later told me that she came back four more times and left with another bag full of breadsticks each time.

Well, Dr. Betty and I sat up in that restaurant from noon until dinner, talking, eating, and me crying, because she was getting into my mind and soul. My friends and family know I don't talk about myself, but she made me talk.

I was emotionally and physically recovering from a run-in with Hurricane Marilyn in St. Thomas. I wasn't the Von that people knew; my spirit was shattered because I had lost everything except my life. Little did I know that this beautiful, giving woman would psychoanalyze me and help me to realize that the hurricane was a closed chapter in my life. "Get over it! You are alive!!" she said. And she went on, telling me, "Discipline of yourself is absolutely necessary before the power of God is given to you. When you see the power of God manifested in others, you do not see the work that has gone before. Find the good and praise it." She said that I was not meant to stay in St. Thomas, that my time there was just a retreat for God to get my attention so he could direct me on the path he wanted me to go and remind me to love myself.

Looking me dead in the eyes, in the hush of that affluent, big-money restaurant, Dr. Betty said, "You do what you have to do. You pick yourself up, make a plan, and work your plan like somebody crazy. You cry, pray, and keep walking toward your dream. You don't depend on wishy-washy folks. You work as if your new life depends on it, 'cause it does." That was it. That hard-willed, I've-been-there-and-back-and-life-is-sweet-and-getting-sweeter philosophy was what held her together. And it was the glue that riveted everybody in their seats at this big church full of folks like me, all thanking God for Betty and the life she breathed into our lives.

It was at the funeral services that I saw the true meaning of *sister-friends*. These powerful and outstanding women came together to show their love and, in front of the world, make a commitment to form an alliance with her children. I wondered if my girlfriends and I have culti-vated that kind of relationship, or if I was witnessing the end of an era. That frightened me. So I called my entertainment-commission buddies and asked each what she thought of the idea of writing a book about Dr. Betty as a tribute from her sisterfriends. Next, I called Dr. Tucker, who said that it was a fabulous idea, but wondered who I would get to write such a book. I said maybe Jamie Foster Brown from *Sister 2 Sister;* Dr. Tucker said she loved Jamie's writing. I called Jamie, and naturally she started whining about her magazine deadlines, but when I told her we could give some money to the Shabazz daughters from us, that this could be part of the beginning of a "Love Is Action" campaign (thanks, Dr. Jenkins), she folded. And this book is the result.

I was always very curious about what Betty Shabazz was like as a child. I set my cousin free in Detroit to find out where she came from and who she was.

Betty grew up in Detroit with her adopted family, the Malloys, and in 1952 graduated from Northern High School, where she was in the French Club, the Nurses Club, and played snare drums in the orchestra. Suesetta McCree was Betty's girlhood friend, Irmagene Graves her high school friend, and Ameenah Omar her sister-in-law. Aunt Ruthie was one of the greatest sources of family strength to Betty and her girls, dispensing food, spankings, and whatever else was needed. We were able to get Betty's school photo, but her friends and family offer the clearest picture of her.

[SUESETTA MCCREE *is a retired sociology professor. She taught at Wayne State University in Detroit.*]

WHEN you really think about it, I knew her well. But how much is there to say? She was younger than me; she was in her early teens when we met. I was in college, so maybe she was fourteen or fifteen. She had come to live with the Malloys. They lived at 313 Hague and I lived at 312. Neighborhoods were different then—a person associated with their neighbors. On that particular street there was a lot of sitting on porches.

The Malloys went to Bethel AME church, and so did I. I went to the Sunday school and often rode with them. Betty was a good girl. She did what she was supposed to. She made good grades in school. She used to go with me to choir practice and she sang with the choir—we were in what they called the youth choir at Bethel. She always went to Sunday school. The church back then had a lot of activities for young people, so we were there most of the day on Sunday. Then on Thursdays, we'd go to choir rehearsal and hang around. There were boys at the church that she liked and there were boys at her school that she liked. But she wasn't a little chatterbox about boys. She talked about other girls, but not in a jealous way. She would talk about some of the girls and what they were doing, but it was not gossipy. These were girls she admired. She'd come over to my house, and we used to bake cookies and listen to records. She did a real interesting dance where everything moved. It was like she was on a string; all her joints moved. It was sort of like the slop, but this was before that dance came out.

Betty and I had some things in common—I guess we related to church. In school, I was a Delta, and she became a Delsprite. Deltas were advisors to the Delsprites. We were sort of a service organization, but also a social organization. I remember taking Betty to one of the Delta parties when she was a Delsprite. To become a member of the Deltas, you had to be invited. A member invited you to a tea party, where they told you what being a Delta was all about and then you were invited to join. Betty was well liked. She became a Delta, and she was also in Jack and Jill of America and was a Link.

She didn't talk about her biological mother, Mrs. Sanders, very much. She called Mrs. Malloy "madear." Mrs. Malloy was very instrumental in the Housewives' League and the credit union at Bethel AME Church. The Malloys were active in Sunday school, and I'm certain Mr. Malloy was an officer of the church. They were upstanding in the community.

Mrs. Malloy sent Betty to Tuskegee. After that, Betty went to New York to school. When she was at Tuskegee, my sister was there. Betty used to go over to her house and use my sister's sewing machine. Betty was quite a seamstress. She could sew and make her own clothes.

Years later, we became quite close. It was very interesting, because I went to graduate school in New York. While I was there, she invited me to her home. She said, "You know what I am," and I said, "You are Betty, my friend." She said, "Okay." She told me how to get to her house, and then she met me at the train. At that time, she had only two children and was pregnant with the third. We went to her home, where she told me that she could have had someone pick me up at my apartment, but she wanted this to be her day, her business. She said they would have talked, they would have said that she was meeting with a devil—a devil, because I was fair skinned. I got to her home, which was lovely. In every room there was a picture of Elijah Muhammad. I had lunch there, and she told me why she had served what she did: lamb, some kind of grapefruit, and some kind of salad. She told me what all of this meant, why they went together. She prayed with her hands up, not together, not closing out a blessing, but open, so you could receive a blessing. It was a very interesting afternoon.

I went out that evening with a young man. I told him I went to the home of a Muslim, my friend from Detroit. And he said, "Oh, did she say anything about Malcolm X?"

I said, "Well, it was Malcolm X's house."

[AUNT RUTH SUMMERFORD *is a retired registered nurse.*]

BETTY was my father's great-niece. My father was William Summerford, and his nephew was Shelman Sandlin, Betty's father. When Betty came to New York for nursing school, her father made sure she got in touch with me because I was living in New York at the time and always tried to keep up with the family. She trained at Brooklyn State Hospital and visited me two or three times a week, plus we spent weekends together. During the time when Betty was in doing some of her training at Montefiore Hospital, she went to Nation of Islam meetings with one of her classmates, who was a Muslim. At one of the meetings, she met Malcolm. After she met Malcolm, she started dating him or being friendly with him. I think she fell in love with him the first time she met him. So she went over to the Muslim faith. When she graduated from Brooklyn State Hospital, they married. He was thirty-two, she was twenty-three.

After Malcolm was killed, I was called up to Sidney Poitier's house in Mount Pleasant. I went up there, and they had a big celebration for Betty. There were quite a few people out doing fund-raising for Betty after Malcolm was killed. I don't know whether Sidney was there in the house or not, or whether his first wife, Juanita, was there either. I remember her because I had spoken to her. Some others who were involved with Betty at the time were Ruby Dee and her husband.

Well, Betty was all right. She was a little standoffish, keeping a watchful eye. At that time she was pregnant with the twins. She did not cry. If she did, she wouldn't let you see it.

I was there for every last one of those girls' births. I was working in maternity at that particular time. They were easy births, with the exception of the twins. The twins were the biggest babies that she had, and they were the ones that she was in the longest labor with.

Betty had a registered nurse's license, but she didn't work as a nurse while Malcolm was living. Later, she had to get back into the workforce, to get her financial standards up. Her having a registered nurse's license meant that she didn't have to work full time, but she worked what we called per diem for so many days a week. She could just about set her own time. So after she started as a nurse, I think she worked about a year or so until somebody offered her some scholarship funds. That's when she went back into education. I was taking care of the kids the whole time. I was up to her house every week. She did have a few housekeepers; I didn't take care of the girls full time—I was there when the housekeeper couldn't be.

Them girls were some real rascals. The point is, they knew everybody around them. They had teenage neighbors beside them, and they would fill in when Betty had to come to the city. They would come over or the girls would go over to their house and stay. There were always children around, like Nina Simone's daughter who was at their house all the time. Those children spent many weekends here with me. They were practically raised here on Pacific Street in Brooklyn. Some of the kids that knew them then still ask me about them every now and again.

[
A M E E N A H   O M A R *is the retired dean of Highland Community College. She served on the Detroit City Council.*
]

I'M Dr. Ameenah Omar. I am the sister-in-law of the late, great Dr. Betty Shabazz. I was married to Malcolm's older brother, El Hajj Abdul Aziz Omar. His given name was Philbert. All of Malcolm's brothers were at one time actively involved in the Nation. Malcolm was an El Hajj, and my husband was an El Hajj. "El Hajj" is an honorific title given to male Muslims who make the pilgrimage to Mecca. A female is an "El Hajji."

My husband passed three years ago. I've grown a lot since then, and I'm just so thankful to have been married to him and to have been in the family. It is a very special family, which I am very proud to be a part of. I admired Betty as a woman—and I like to use the term *woman* when I refer to her. Because in my mind the difference between a woman and a lady is that a lady acts a certain way all the time, and a woman does what she has to do when she has to do it with whatever means she has available. Sister Betty always represented that to me. My appreciation for her started long before I became a member of the family.

My one regret, which I no longer have and my husband came to terms with before he died, is that he was very active in the Nation of Islam at the time that Malcolm was assassinated. Abdul was summoned to Chicago—he thought he was going to see the Honorable Elijah Muhammad (may Allah forgive him his sins), but when he got there, there was this huge press conference going on. Just as they went on the air, the brothers told him he was on and handed him a script. When he started to read from it, he realized that the script was condemning Malcolm. And that plagued my husband for a long, long time.

This was after Malcolm died, after he was assassinated. Abdul didn't leave the Nation after Malcolm was assassinated, like Betty did. His reconciliation had nothing to do with anybody else. In Islam, your reconciliation is between you and God. My husband and the rest of Malcolm's family were very clear that the brothers in the Nation of Islam had Malcolm killed. They believed that this was done with the permission and consent of the U.S. government because it fit in with their own plan. The brothers who actually committed the act, though, had been made to believe that it was *jihad*, that this would ensure their place in heaven. *Jihad* is committing an act that the perpetrator feels will ensure his place in paradise.

My husband was a very wise and good man. He recognized that there are people who become so powerful in what they are doing that they can manipulate the emotions of others. I think that one reason that he could come to terms with what happened is because he embraced traditional Islam. In traditional Islam, Orthodox Islam, which is what the Honorable Elijah Muhammad told us we would get later, we understand that when one asks to be forgiven for an act, one is always forgiven.

I, as a family member, am a Pan-African woman who is real clear about her Kujichagulia. I decide who I am, I will speak for myself. One of the people who inspired me to be so clear about my role as a black woman was Dr. Betty Shabazz. I'm going to tell you that this had nothing to do with us being in the same family—it had to do with Betty being who she was. Betty defined herself, she spoke for herself, she never tried to be Mrs. Malcolm X, and I mean that as no disrespect to the sisters who are carrying on their brothers' teaching. I mean it to say that Betty was an example to us all.

Betty's attitude was, "My husband was not the first husband in the struggle who lost his life. I'm a woman. I have these children to raise and this is what I have to do."

She didn't lay back and say, "Oh I have to go on welfare because they killed my husband." That would have been repeating what is a pattern in the family. The pattern in the sense that my mother-in-law—Malcolm's mother—lived through all those horrendous acts perpetrated by mixed-up, misguided Europeans and mixed-up, misguided people of color against her husband and her family. After her husband was killed, she refused to talk to white people, and for that she was put in a mental hospital. So the children had to get in the system, adult care and welfare. Sister Betty never did that. She raised her children, she went back to school, and she began to share who she was as a person. And there's a lesson in that for all of us, in my opinion, having experienced some of the things that Sister Betty experienced. Whether it was our grand-fathers, our uncles, or our cousins, we had to take a lesson from her. Those things happened, yes, and we must never forget it, but we must look for the good and praise it. Look for the good and celebrate it. In that we have a heritage of goodness. Even when we are misguided, we still have the potential for doing right.

Betty, at a time when women were subservient in the Nation of Islam, when women were supposed to be covered up, refused to do that. She refused to look anything but beautiful. She was beautiful and she wanted to look that way. My husband also said that Betty had a very strong streak of independence, that she was not going to refuse to say some-thing because she was a woman or because she was Malcolm's wife. She still had her opinions, and she did not hesitate to share those opinions whenever she got the opportunity. Betty was adored by her adopted parents and never had to want for anything, and suddenly she was mar-ried to a high-profile man who gave everything to the Nation. If the truth be told, the greatest growth in the Nation of Islam occurred as a result of Malcolm. Malcolm had a strong attraction for men, to men, by men. Because they saw themselves in him. Black men throughout history have always had strong feelings about freedom. Strong feelings about protecting their families. Strong feelings about the role that the man played, but because of the circumstances of our experience in this coun-try, they weren't able to articulate those feelings like Malcolm did. So Malcolm spoke for them.

ℬ

I remember my husband telling me about how Malcolm and Betty got married. Malcolm was a young minister, and ministers needed to be married. In Islam, you know, it is natural for a man and a woman to be together. There is a strong sense of responsibility for nation building. At the same time that Malcolm and the family had Islam, they came from an environment where their mother was a follower of Marcus Garvey. Their father, while he was a minister, was also one steeped in the greatness of blackness. So they grew up hearing their mother always telling them stories about their uncles who were kings and their aunts who were queens and what a great heritage they had. My husband said that he was an adult before he realized that he didn't have uncles named King Philbert or King Wilfred. That's the environment that they came from.

I think Malcolm was maybe seven and my husband nine when their father was killed. Abdul said that Malcolm had a severe reaction to that. Malcolm was very bright; he was an A-student in school. But when this happened to their father, Malcolm began to act out his feelings, which is not uncommon for a young man. And Malcolm had this other experience that Abdul described to me that he thought was a turning point: Malcolm wanted to be a lawyer. One day he told them that the school counselor had told him that he would never be a lawyer because Negroes couldn't be lawyers. The counselor told him he needed to go to a vocational school. When the family was separated, Malcolm was put in the home of a white couple in Mason, Michigan. Here you have this bright young boy who has a sense of who he is as a black man, put into the home of white folks. It breaks your heart.

I personally met Betty at my mother-in-law's funeral. That is one of my very fond memories. She was very particular about her appearance. If you look at pictures of her in the Nation, you would see her hair. At that time we weren't supposed to show it, but you saw Betty's hair. She was gorgeous.

Women in the mosque were seen but not heard. In terms of being different and demanding a change, women didn't speak. They were seen, but they were like children. Malcolm would call my husband and say, "Boy, Betty was out at MGT"—Muslim Girls Training, that's what it was called then—"She caused a stir today because she had a lot to say." Malcolm was struggling with that. He had to deal with this. He had this wife at home that he cherished and adored for her mind and everything. They couldn't chastise her because she was married to the minister. Which again goes back to her seeing her role and defining herself.

I think history was one of the reasons I was really happy to be a part of this project. Because Betty in her own right was as much a catalyst for change for women in the Nation as much as Malcolm was for the men. She was so unassuming in terms of wanting the spotlight on herself. She acted out who she was without fanfare, which in my opinion gives another example to those of us who are married to high-profile men. We don't have to try to overshadow him or outdo him; we have to make a difference where we are with what we have. That difference will only complement what our husbands are doing. Betty never walked behind Malcolm or anything like that. I'm sure there were people that were bothered by it, and it would be naïve of me to assume that they were not because I'm sure they were.

BETTY'S last public appearance was here in Detroit at the Malcolm X Academy. She helped them to launch their fund-raising initiative to take some children to Africa. After her accident I decided I wasn't going to let it fail. I stepped in to make sure the family was represented, and I even took the trip, because she loved that academy. That's why I really want to emphasize to you that Betty's mark on my life and many other women of colors' lives was not directly related to Malcolm. I certainly don't mean to take anything away from him, I don't mean that at all. What I mean to say is that Betty was a great person in her own right. We need to tell the story of sisters who are great in their own right so that we can have sheroes.

[
IRMAGENE GRAVES *was a childhood friend of
Dr. Betty Shabazz. She lives in Detroit.*
]

BETTY lived in Detroit with Mr. and Mrs. Malloy, who adopted her. We were childhood friends. She was a young teenager when I met her. Her family belonged to Bethel AME Baptist Church. I lived on Alger and she lived on Hague. Betty started coming to Bethel with Mr. and Mrs. Malloy. They asked us to be friends with her and told us they were adopting her. Mrs. Malloy wanted her to meet—as they said back then—some nice teenagers. Betty was very nice. We never really talked much about her background. Once in a while she would mention a few things, but we never pursued it further. You know how kids are—when you are compatible, you don't worry about much else.

I remember her saying she was running with the wrong crowd of kids in Detroit on the East Side. She used to say that they got bored and would make nonsense calls to people and hang up. She showed me how they did it. They would go through the telephone book at random. Page by page and just call people. Another thing with Betty was that she had a little strut to her step. You know how they used to walk. It was like saying, "they're bad" and "they're in the know." Which these days is so minor. She had a little strut, but it was a little more sophisticated. I used to say, "Girl, you can strut!"

Betty was a smart girl, and she was very likable. We made friends very easily. She was just like the other kids, nothing out of the ordinary. She wore regular clothes and saddle oxfords. The hair was the same as you see in the pictures. She never changed her hair.

Betty liked boys then, but she wasn't wild about them. We were more on the tame and somewhat quiet side. We double-dated a few times, but this one time made us laugh every time we remembered it. You see, there was a fellow who took me out one evening who brought along a friend. They wanted to know if I had a girlfriend. So I asked Betty.

The four of us went to a show and then out to eat. Betty loved shrimp, and I remember we ended up going to Dot and Etta's Shrimp Hut. The fellow with Betty said he didn't want any shrimp. (That's what made it so funny.) The two fellows went and got the shrimp for us to share, and when they got back in the car, Betty figured out that her date had been eating some of the shrimp. All of a sudden Betty said, "That's your last one." Everybody stopped talking and looked at her. Betty said, "You didn't want any, but now you are eating them too fast." Betty wouldn't let anyone get over on her — not even in those days.

*Betty did the electric slide. Oh, my God, I didn't know
she did the electric slide. Betty went bowling. Betty
liked to have a good time. The living-large Betty. One
thing all of her friends talked about was that
she led a full life.*

**When you start to peel away the different layers of Betty
Shabazz's life, you discover that Betty is 007. Every woman
should be able to live a life as full as Dr. Shabazz's was. She
was comical, she was shrewd, she was smart, she was playful.
She remembered her relationships, and she didn't mix them.
She kept everything in her life compartmentalized.**

*I think you will find some contradicting stories as
you move forward in this book but that was who
she was. Some people will say, "Betty never did
that"—and others will reply, "Yes, she did."*

RUTH CLARK *owns CUP Temporaries, Inc., and is president of the Support Network, Inc., in New York City.*

I'M Ruth Clark, president and CEO of CUP Temporaries, Inc., and founding president of the Support Network, Inc. Betty's daughter, Qubilah, works with us. She did not need to be home alone brooding after the death of her mother. She needed to remain occupied and liked the idea of working with the Support Network because of its involvement in minority affairs. She has been through a lot of tragedies but she is proving herself to be strong and very resilient—like her mother.

Qubilah's son, Malcolm, is doing quite well. He is a brilliant youngster who enjoys reading. This young man did not intentionally burn his grandmother. Malcolm is at the top of all his classes. I know that his grandmother, Betty, is looking down from heaven and she must be happy to see his progress. You know . . . God works in mysterious ways—unfortunately, sometimes we don't understand his agenda.

I met Betty back in the early seventies, long after Malcolm was killed. Years later, Betty brought one of her twins, Malaak, to work for me. She was fifteen or sixteen years old. She said to Malaak, "This is going to be your second mom." I don't know why she brought Malaak to me, I never asked. Malaak's the only one that she brought down at the time. I always wanted to meet her twin sister, Malikah, but I didn't at that time. After Malaak graduated from high school and went on to college, I hired her to do a project for me.

Betty and I remained very good friends. I would just listen when she wanted to talk. Sometimes I would offer advice, but mostly I was there to listen. I would talk to her, and I would tell her if I thought some things were just. She would listen. Sometimes when people want to talk they are not interested in criticism. They are not interested in your comments. They just want a shoulder to lean on. Sometimes Betty would call me very early in the morning or very late at night just to talk. She wanted to talk when things were troubling her, and I would listen. That was the friendship we had.

Betty never talked about remarrying, because she was still in love with Malcolm. She never dealt with Malcolm being dead. She'd always refer to him in the present tense. The girls told me the same thing — that she always spoke of him in the present. I think she did a hell of a lot with the cards she was dealt.

I was featured in a book, back in the mid-eighties, *Women Making History*. When they asked me who my role model was I said unequivocally, "Betty Shabazz." From then on she loved me to death. After that, I couldn't get rid of her. She said, "Well, girl, since I'm your role model, you have to go everywhere with me." One thing that was wonderful about her is that she would always introduce you to people from everywhere. She would say, "You must meet my friend Ruth Clark. She runs a personnel agency and she takes care of my daughter. It's not about me, it's about Ruth Clark. You must meet my friend Ruth Clark."

My organization gave Betty an award three years ago. She was so touched by it and the kids loved it. This one little boy asked her to dance. It was the cutest little thing. He came up to her and said, "Ms. Shabazz, would you dance with me?" And she looked and said, "Certainly, Darling." And they were moving around the floor. It was so cute.

I went out with Betty to her Links dance three weeks before the tragedy. She was involved with the Links chapter up in Westchester County, New York. I believe it was on May 10, 1997. She was so full of life that night. She was doing the macarena and the electric slide. I would never get on the floor with her. She was light on her feet. I'd say, "Betty, I am not dancing." But she did thank me for allowing her to dance with my husband. She had the most wonderful time and she was so full of life. She was wearing one of her St. John's knits which she used to wear well.

It's just the weirdest thing. That night she started telling me this stuff. She was just venting about everything. She started answering questions that I had always had in my mind, that I had never had the nerve to ask. And I asked myself why she was telling me all this.

I still have not come to terms with her death. The girls are very strong. They made all the decisions in regards to the funeral. In fact, they were the last to see her. The cleansing process—they did it all by themselves. They put oil on the body and they wrapped her in a shroud. The night she died, I saw her go to heaven. The funny thing is, Malaak told me she saw the same thing. I was on my terrace and Malaak was on her fire escape. She said, "I saw my mother." I said, "I saw her too." She saw her slowly going up and when she got to the sky, she just flew in. It was as if Malcolm reached out and said, "Come on in here, girl." She was flying up very slowly like a bird. It was beautiful. And it seems like he reached out and got her. I'll never forget it.

EVELYN CUNNINGHAM *is a recipient of the prestigious George Pope Award for Journalism. A former newspaper journalist in New York City, she is cofounder of New York's flagship chapter of the Coalition of 100 Black Women. She was also the special assistant to Governor Rockefeller and director of the New York State Women's Division.*

FOR twenty-five years I was a journalist with the *Pittsburgh Courier.* That was the largest and most powerful black newspaper in the world during the fifties, sixties, and seventies. I also helped create the New York chapter of the Coalition of 100 Black Women. Malcolm and I met when I was with the *Pittsburgh Courier.* My first job was in the *Courier*'s New York office, which was on 125th Street, Malcolm was always on 125th Street at the corner making a speech. That's when he was a street-corner rouser. He often stopped in my office, and for a couple of years we were friends. He would stop by, and when I didn't have a real exciting lead story, I would say, "Malcolm, say something, give me something. Give me a quote so I can get a story moving." He would laugh about it. I think he liked me and had respect for me. I certainly liked him, but the respect at that point was not quite in full bloom because I had not yet started to take him seriously, even though I thought he was a very interesting young man.

I knew he had a wife, and I begged him many times to let me interview her, because I was so curious about the fact that he was married and the kind of woman he would be married to. And I wanted to hear from her, how much she shared his philosophies. He kept promising me that one day I would meet her and I could do a story on her. He did at one point say, "Well, I am going to let you meet Betty and talk with her." And I was ecstatic—I told my home office that I was going to meet Betty Shabazz and it's going to be something special; let's get ready. At this time Malcolm X was pretty universally known. But the next day after Malcolm told me that, a story about Betty appeared on the front page of another paper—I think it was the *Herald Tribune*. I was devastated. I thought he had deceived me. I was so upset I didn't know what to do, and my story never got written. I was angry, but we never talked about it.

I did not actually meet Betty until after Malcolm was killed. When Betty and I first met, she was very warm and almost welcomed my bringing up what was bothering me. She knew the whole story. She told me many times that her husband talked about me all the time. And she said, "I didn't know if I was going to get ready to hate you, but I don't think I hate you, you seem to be okay."

My analysis of Betty's statement was that she probably had a wee bit of envy of me as a working woman. As I got to know her, I decided that she would tell a lady to work and not to be the type of wife that she had been. I think that she would have liked to be a newspaper person, or anything out there meeting people. I'm guessing on that, but when I think I'm right, I think I'm right. I think she wanted more out of life than being a cook and a mother.

We had an immediate attraction. I liked Betty immediately and she seemed to like me. When she asked me about her husband—this really put me at ease—she asked me, "Were you fooling around with my husband?" I said, "Hell no! He was a hero, and you don't mess around with heroes. At least I don't." We joked about that in different ways very often and I felt good to be able to do that.

I was not a close, close friend. I was one of the "hey, girlfriends." You know her phrase. That's what she called everybody, all the women when she called them up. She would say, "Hey, girlfriend."

Betty and I both got involved in a gourmet club, so we saw each other fairly regularly. It's a group of about eight, brought together by Lena McPhatter-Gore, the widow of the great jazz musician Clyde McPhatter.

Really, though, we chose each other. Lena happens to be an excellent, excellent gourmet cook. One of the greatest. We were sitting around— Lena and I and one other person—talking about the possibility of just getting together and cooking. We thought we'd limit it to a small group, but I think it ended up being eight. My turn to cook would come up only once a year, which was more than enough. We'd plan, and it got to be so funny. For instance, when it was my turn and we were sitting around the table and I had to write the menu down, somebody would tell me, "I think it's got too much oregano" or "this wine really does not lend itself to this meal." We would be very critical. It was very funny. We were very serious about gourmet food. And we would serve it up beautifully, no such thing as paper napkins.

We went up to Betty's house up in Mount Vernon. It was a big, lovely house. The girls were around, but we didn't see much of them. They were ducking in and out. I don't remember what the side dishes were, but I remember that the main dish was chicken. She had candlelight and all those other kinds of things. The food was pretty good. Not great like Lena's or a couple of the other women's, which was super—people like Betty and me were struggling.

We'd talk about fun things. About men. She would kid me, "You always got some man with you." I'd say, "Betty, this man, I think, is going to be my husband; now don't say that." "Where do you find these men? Do you know any young men," she'd ask? We laughed and joked about that.

Betty loved to dance; she was an excellent dancer—ballroom dancing. She was just good at it; she was so light on her feet, and here she is a heavy woman. She and a man named Malcolm Corrin. I watched them at a couple of affairs, at dinner dances, and they just glided across the floor, dipping and swaying. She loved all those social things. I think I heard the oldest daughter say that Malcolm was a good dancer too. I think she was talking about her father dancing around the house. They probably danced a lot.

ℬ

BETTY had a look that was all her own. She dressed conservatively, but she was inclined to be a little bit sexy, tight around the top. She was heavy, but never very heavy. I would see her at the fund-raisers: the NAACP fund-raiser, the Urban League; all of these people and a lot of clubs, and they all have an annual fund-raiser. And you see usually the same people at all of them. There would be a reunion-type atmosphere and they were a lot of fun. Betty was a giving woman. The last time I saw her was at Sylvia's restaurant. We were there with Al Sharpton. We sat around there for three or four hours, yacking and having fun. I'm glad we had that last time together.

[BARBARA DANIEL COX *is a self-employed business woman who produces special events in Philadelphia.*]

I met Betty in January 1985, in Nairobi, Kenya. A group of African American women were meeting with the planning committee in Kenya in preparation for the United Nations Decade for Women Conference and the Nongovernmental Organization (NGO) forum. I happened to be the only one who was not a national leader — I was head of the mayor's commission for women in Philadelphia. The trip to Kenya was an opportunity for African American women to interact with their sisters who were planning and would be hosting this event.

One of the things I remember most vividly was Betty when a group of us traveled to an area outside of Nairobi — to a countryside where there were thousands of people gathered. When they introduced the widow of Malcolm X, the people went wild. Betty got a stronger response than President Daniel arap Moi. They were wild just to know she was there, because they loved Malcolm. To know that his wife was in their presence was almost like having him. She was humbled. She was pleased, and I think she was a little surprised that people received her that well. Some of her issue was that America didn't accept Malcolm as well until it became popular to say you were somebody that supported Malcolm and appreciated him. So she was humbled by that and really appreciative.

We were together again in July, during the conference. A year later, we sponsored a follow-up session in Philadelphia and Betty was one of our guests. Then we coordinated an International Women's Conference in 1987 reflecting on what had happened after the world conference in July. Betty and I became friendly because I started getting her speaking engagements in and around Philadelphia. We became telephone buddies and we sometimes spent time together at the Congressional Black Caucus.

One of the places that she went to with me was a club in Philadelphia named Big Will's. There was a birthday party for Tim Spencer, a friend of mine who was the head of the Philadelphia Anti-Graffiti Network. Betty had met Tim when they did a tribute to Malcolm, a three-story wall mural. Betty came to that ceremony. I have pictures of her in front of the mural and with people who came to the event. Betty appreciated him because he thought enough of her husband to create a memorial to him. I remember Betty calling Tim to say she was ready to have the photos. She called him and said she was catching a train and would be stopping in Philadelphia on her way someplace else but not leaving the train station. She asked him to meet her at the train station and deliver the photos to her so she wouldn't have to wait. She would find a way to get what she wanted when she wanted it. And she was comfortable asking anybody for it.

Now back to Big Will's, which was what we used to call a "corner." It was a neighborhood establishment, and the people who were there were people without titles. They were neighborhood people, because that's who was important to Tim. I don't remember why she was in town, but I was taking her back to a late train. And I said that Tim would love it if she would stop in at this party. When I walked in there with her, the people went crazy because they just could not believe she'd come. They started taking pictures, they started asking for her autograph, to sit and talk with her, to take pictures with her. I mean, people were just crazy.

When she got up to do the electric slide in the line with everybody, they just could not believe it. I don't know how she learned it, but she knew it. And it was the highlight of a lot of people's lives because they touched her, they danced with her, they were on the floor with her, they were in a picture with her. It was just great. She laughed and had fun.

Betty liked to bowl, too. I found that out through her grandson Malcolm. He used to visit with me some holidays, and, in fact, he stayed with me for a little while in 1995. Betty came in one weekend to be with him and they went to a bowling party. She was just so excited. Sometimes I would go to meet her at the train station, and I remember one time she was an hour late because she was bowling. She couldn't pull herself away from bowling.

ॐ

I remember Betty used to always tell me to make sure that my Delta dues were paid. She was a Delta. She was a Link. In fact, the Deltas honored her at their national convention—two of her daughters were there to accept the award. One of the things she did every year was the National Black Holistic Society Kwanzaa Retreat. She was a really supportive person. If she believed in what people did, she supported them and would go out of her way to make sure that she could be with people. I remember this sister from Decatur, Georgia, who when she had lunch with Betty just cried to be in Betty's presence. She was like, "I can't believe I'm sitting here with you and you're having lunch with us." Betty would say, "Oh child, what are you talking about? Why not?" She developed a relationship with the woman, and the woman was just freaked out.

❦

ONE of the issues Betty had with some men was their problems with her being Malcolm's widow and what they imagined they had to live up to. But it wasn't about living up to Malcolm. I guess it's just that people would be overwhelmed to see her, to be able to sit at a table with her.

I remember Betty coming to one of my Malcolm X ceremonies here in Philadelphia when a little young girl had won this contest speaking about Malcolm and Martin. This was in May, for Malcolm's birthday. I did my program one day and Betty did her program the next. She liked this girl so much, she said, "Barbara, you have to bring her to New York tomorrow and put her on my program." I remember that it was snowing that day. I had to get the girl's teacher and mother, and we took that little girl up there to be on Betty's program. Another year, a sister named Rose Samuels did a piece on Malcolm, and Betty liked her so much that we brought her up too.

❦

ONE time, she met my cousin, Renee, who had on a fur coat that she had gotten from a recycled-fur shop. And Betty said, "Take me to the place where your cousin got that fur. Do you know where it is?" I took her, she ordered a fur, paid for it, and told them to inscribe her name in it in red and that she needed it in an hour because she had to catch a train. These poor people are going crazy because there was no way that they can get it done in an hour, because they had to send it out to get her name monogrammed in it, but she just leaned and leaned and leaned until she finally had to catch the train. And she said to me, "You go back there and get my coat and you Express Mail it to me overnight. I want that coat tomorrow." That is another example of Betty getting what she wants, when she wants it. She had the fur the next day.

> PATRICIA RUSSELL MCCLOUD *is the national president of the Links, Inc.*

THE Links, Inc., is a by-invitation organization. Chapter members — wherever they are based — identify a woman in their area who in their view is service-minded, is willing to give service to her community, then they take her through orientation and vote her in. We teach service — that this is going to take some of your time, some of your talent, some of your resources, some of your connections, and you will become a part of a cadre of capable, committed, and long-serving women. Now, if you're not serious about that, then don't do it, because that is our mission. We are supposed to be more than check-writing folks who sit back and say, "I'm a Link." We volunteer.

Sara Strickland-Scott and Margaret Hawkins cofounded the Links on November 9, 1946, in Philadelphia. They were two women who felt that as physicians' wives, they did not do enough for the community. Margaret Hawkins said, "You know, I'm wondering — if we had some friends over and talked to them about giving more service, more structured service to the community, would they come?" And so Sara said, "I think so," and nine other women joined them. They said, "Well we could have a meeting, and after the meeting, since many of our husbands are doctors and we don't get to see them as much after work as we might like, we could have a dinner." The men originally were called "Missing Links," but ultimately they became known as "Connecting Links." They met those eleven women. The children became "Heir-O-Links." The girls ultimately had the opportunity to become Links.

It was requested that I consider Betty for membership. She was brought to my attention as a person that might be a good candidate to be the director of International Trends and Services. That is a major program for the Links. I gave her that appointment for the years 1994 through 1996. I think that what was stated at the time was that she would bring a lot to the table because of her involvement internationally and domestically in the large network of individuals with whom she served on boards, in associations, and in groups. Organizationally, we have programmed quite successfully in the areas of youth, the arts, and national trends and services—the Links' other three program facets—but we are not always as successful in our international programs. So that's how Betty was introduced to me—as a person who could dig deeper programmatically.

Betty to me was a very contemplative, deliberative person who had good thoughts and strong thoughts, who had a sense of institutionalism, and a sense of history. She was very, very cognizant that her whole network of people was atypical for anyone—I mean, even the most exposed person would not have the considerable network of high-level people that she enjoyed and was included in. That was certainly a joy for her. I really was constantly aware that Betty enjoyed, appreciated, accepted, and anticipated being within the embrace of that network of friends, acquaintances, and colleagues.

She never seemed particularly humorous until one night when the board members were relaxing. Annual board meetings are always intense—very focused and fast moving—and afterward we have dinner. Then we may go to the suites, and you just have cathartic release talk about how you're doing, what you're doing, and all that. I had never seen Betty be funny—she was the funniest person that night. I thought I was going to faint. Someone asked her, "What do you do if your guy goes away and doesn't live up to your expectations? How do you handle it?" And she said, "There is nothing to do but find you another one." We said, "What!?" We had kind of tiptoed around that subject forever; at least, I never would talk about remarriage or a b-person because of the revered status of Malcolm in everybody's mind. So you just tiptoed around second marriages or renewal or "seek and find." Never, never would we—but when Betty said that, we said, "Oh, then we *can* talk about this." She said it with a smile. People thought it was just amazing. It was refreshing.

When the Links, Inc., was founded, it was not meant to be a huge organization or an organization that people can join on a whim. Now, I'm giving you this history in these few lines just so you'll appreciate what happened when Betty died. Margaret Hawkins and Sara Strickland-Scott wanted to ensure that this organization was a chain of friends who were linked one to another, that there would be a heart-to-heart, breast-to-breast connection, as we were sisters linked to the chain. They wanted to be sure everyone knew who you were and who your children were. Everybody was in a loop of caring and sharing.

So when the news of Betty Shabazz's misfortune hit Linkdom, not only we as a people, as a black people, but we as an organization of sisters, were devastated.

We felt the need to come together to ascertain what we would do now and how we would do it as one. To embrace again, because we are family. I don't remember where I was in my schedule, but I do remember that my schedule was completely altered for me to come to New York for the memorial. I remember being in the Atlanta airport, and Eugene Jackson and Phyllis, his wife, were en route. We were on the same flight and took the same limo along with Dr. Marcella Maxwell, who is the Links' NGO (Nongovermental Organization) representative to the United Nations. We then rode to the church. There were throngs of people, throngs of people. All of us came together and commiserated over the loss. It was standing-room only—the church must have held three thousand people. Every speaker knew a different Betty. There was some commonality, but there were some also obvious differences as to who she was, how she was, and what she did, but everyone agreed that she was always giving of herself. If you were in her walk, if you were in her project, you knew she'd give it her all. She was, perhaps like all of us, a work in progress. Now that her work is finished . . . ours must continue.

[ToNI FAY *is vice president for Community Relations at Time Warner, Inc.*]

I met Betty during what I'd call our family retreat—a women's issues–oriented forum in New York. (This year will be our fifteenth or sixteenth retreat.) I really got to know Betty, and I would see her all around because of the type of work I do. I was always in awe of her accomplishments and how a woman left to raise all those children could live and keep it so together. When I met her, Betty was trying to complete a book about Malcolm. And that was very difficult for her.

She was working on that book, but she could not get the story told. I remember staying up with her one night very, very late. It was me, Betty, and Minyon Moore, and we talked about what that book should be and how she should approach it; she wanted our ideas. And I spent so much time with her—that's when I learned about her love for Malcolm and how difficult it was and how much the people who helped her then meant to her, because they weren't a popular family. I learned who had helped when there was no help, and who had helped when Malcolm died, and who paid for the funeral. We talked about the people. She should have dedicated the book to them.

She told us that she was going to start writing because she had started talking to us about how she had to get her children out of there, about the fear, and about how difficult it was and how she would always, always be beholden to the people who helped her through that time. But she said that she was not sure she could finish it, because it was just too painful.

ℬ

ANOTHER side of her psychology was love of "giveaways." Betty loved free stuff. Anytime she'd come to an affair, she'd make sure she got her little—what do you call things people give you?—courtesy baskets. She made sure she had hers and anybody else's. She would not go someplace where they were giving away something and not get hers.

She came as my guest one day to a big luncheon for women. She wanted to start networking with some of the corporate women and to get her daughters to know them. She was always saying to them, I need you to meet this one, I want you to meet that one. We were giving away door prizes and stuff. And she was just mad until her number came up. We had to make sure Betty's number came up. She started winning a lot of things because everybody said to let Betty have it. So somebody said, "When are you going to let me have it?" And Betty said, "Are you kidding? I'm taking all this stuff with me." Boy, she loved free stuff. And she loved hanging out with the women.

ℬ

I remember she made me stay up all night to go with her to the presidential prayer breakfast before Clinton's second inauguration. I said, Betty, I'm not going to the prayer service. We have to get up at six o'clock in the morning. Have you lost it?" Plus the fact that I didn't get any tickets for that because I knew I wasn't going. She said, "Don't worry, I have a ticket."

So she gets me up and we go to the presidential inaugural prayer service. It was at a black church, and not many people could get in. I got up, got dressed, we got picked up. We get there, and Betty has no tickets either! You don't go walking in without clearance from the Secret Service when the president is there. We're walking up and the Secret Service is stopping people right before the church, down the street. I said, "Dr. Shabazz, you don't have any tickets," and people around us are going, "Oh, Dr. Shabazz." So we were able to make our way through. Then, when she was right up by the Secret Service all of a sudden Muslim sisters showed up with two tickets for Betty. Out of the clear blue, here comes two tickets. We not only got in but they sat us in the third row.

[**LENA MCPHATTER-GORE** *is the widow of jazz great Clyde McPhatter.*]

I met Betty at the Coalition of 100 Black Women in 1975. I really got to know her when she joined the gourmet club. The organization was started by Karen Johnson and me. Betty was referred to the group by Jewel Jackson-McCabe.

Betty was reluctant to cook, but she finally did. Her dinner was very nice. We ate at her home in Mount Vernon. She first served hors d'oeuvres and shelled almonds, dried apricots and a glazed mixed fruit in Cointreau liqueur. She also served steamed shrimp. The wine was Chablis blanc, served in slim goblets. This was followed by an array of asparagus, lettuce, artichoke hearts, black olives, and broccoli. She worked hard on it. She made a real big effort to do it and she did. The main course was pineapple Japanese chicken served with natural wild rice. That was followed by a refreshing finale of fresh fruit — cantaloupe, honeydew, and mango. At the end of the evening she gave us each a copy of *How to Survive in New York with Children.*

It was a very interesting book; it told you of all the places you could take your kids. We teased her about how we knew someone had helped her with the dinner, but she just laughed. Betty stayed with the cooking club until June 1978, when she no longer had the time to take her turn when it came up. When we met, we usually talked about food and our children. We didn't really talk about business.

Dr. Shabazz always kept Malcolm's legacy alive. (Photo credit: Anthony Mills Photography)

Betty Sanders graduated from Detroit's Northern High School in 1952. This is her senior class picture. (Photo credit: Northern High School Vikings Yearbook, Detroit, Michigan)

Betty was active in the school orchestra, the nursing club, and, as seen here, the French club at Northern High. (Photo credit: Northern High School Vikings Yearbook, Detroit, Michigan)

Betty, sassy and proud, after graduating from nursing school in Tuskegee. (Photo credit: Suesetta McCree)

Betty with the twins, Malikah and Malaak, who were born after their father's death. (Photo credit: Roy Lewis Photography)

The "Three M's," the widows of Malcolm X, Martin Luther King, and Medgar Evers. Left to right: *Betty Shabazz, Coretta Scott King, and Myrlie Evers-Williams. (Photo credit: Van Evers)*

Dr. Shabazz and her friend Dr. C. DeLores Tucker at the NPCBW tribute to the three widows. (Photo credit: Joe C. Thomas)

Dr. Shabazz and Dr. Niara Sudarkasa, president of Lincoln University. (Photo: courtesy of Niara Sudarkasa)

One of Dr. Shabazz's dearest girlfriends was Laura Ross Brown. (Photo credit: Roy Lewis Photography)

Dr. Shabazz and her friends Coretta Scott King and Dr. Maya Angelou in attendance at the opening of the new center for the National Council of Negro Women. (Photo credit: National Council of Negro Women)

Dr. Dorothy I. Height is president emeritus of the National Council of Negro Women and both worked and shopped alongside Dr. Shabazz for more than two decades. (Photo credit: National Council of Negro Women)

Reverend Willie Barrow, president of the Rainbow Coalition and pastor of the Vernon Park Church of God, accompanied Dr. Shabazz to the 1994 Skinner's Leadership Retreat. (Photo credit: The Rainbow Coalition)

In 1995, two regal women, Dr. Betty Shabazz and Khadijah Jordan Farrakhan, came together again, after thirty years of estrangement, at the "Call for Justice" rally in New York City. (Photo credit: Jamie Foster Brown)

The release of the motion picture Malcolm X *was cause for celebration. Dr. Shabazz congratulates director Spike Lee and Denzel Washington. (Photo credit: Oggi Ogburn)*

Dr. Shabazz was an inspiration to many young people. Here, she's seen with MTV's Ananda Lewis at the 1997 Trumpet Awards. (Photo credit: Mark King)

Among the many friends and loved ones who offered moving tributes to Dr. Shabazz at her memorial service were Ossie Davis and Ruby Dee. (Photo credit: Hakim Mutlaq Photographics)

Dr. Betty and Malcolm's legacy, their daughters. Attallah, the oldest, spoke for them all. (Photo credit: Hakim Mutlaq Photographics)

I was telling a couple of my girlfriends that I was about to begin this book. You can imagine how my mouth fell open when one said that her father saw to it that Malcolm X was properly prepared for burial and the other one said that her father was the accountant for the Honorable Elijah Muhammad. And I said, "Tell me your stories."

Cathy Hughes had me come to her house to hear her story, and I spent the night. Bethann Hardison called up late one night and told her story. It was very difficult for her. But in the end they were very happy to share their stories with us and to be able to share them with Betty.

[CATHY HUGHES *is the president and chief executive officer of Radio One, Inc.*]

A lot of people were not aware that Betty was the second-largest stockholder in Inner City Broadcasting. I was a young woman in radio twenty-five years ago when I managed my first station, and Betty informed me that she was the quiet, second-largest stockholder in Inner City. I was very amazed. I was at an affair, and I walked up and introduced myself to her and told her that I was the general manager of WHUR-FM. She said to me, "You and I need to talk." Usually when you approach individuals like Dr. Betty Shabazz at social gatherings, it's rare that any of them say "we need to talk." Particularly to a young person, and we're talking over twenty years ago. They rarely say "let's get together," they're usually trying to avoid resumes and requests for speaking engagements and all that. I thought it really warm that she would say that to me, but I never once for a moment thought she was serious—I thought it was just conversation. I felt inspired that someone as important as Dr. Betty Shabazz would say that to me.

Well, lo and behold, no more than a week later, my secretary rings me and tells me that Dr. Betty Shabazz is on the phone. Until that moment, I have to admit I was wondering, do I call her? She gave me her business card, didn't write her home number or anything. It was just her business number, and I figured I would never be able to get through. I figured I would just see her again and maybe she would remember me and we would start over again. The first thing out of her mouth was, "I thought, young lady, that you were going to call me." And I said, "Well, I was kind of confused. I didn't know if I should. I didn't know if I could get through." And then I told her, "I'm going to be honest with you, Dr. Shabazz. I thought you were just making conversation." She said, "I don't make conversation."

So we started off our relationship with her putting me in my place. She was reprimanding me very gently. She was saying that when some-one says to you, "You and I should talk," then you as a young professional should take the initiative and follow up on it.

As the years went on, I learned that she always sought out young peo-ple, particularly women, and gave them encouragement. Over the years, I've shared this story with other people and they've said that that's how they met her. She said, "Give me a call." And she was serious about it. She was a great listener. As you were telling your side of the story or ex-plaining, Betty would just listen very attentively and kind of say, "uhm." Just to let you know that she was paying attention, but she didn't interject or interrupt. It reminded me very much of generations past, our ances-tors, our great-grandmothers. She asked me about myself. What were my career goals? How was I going to do the job? After I hung up from that first conversation, I was really glowing because she and I had bonded im-mediately. She was surprised to find out that I had known Malcolm.

My father had been an accountant for the Honorable Elijah Muham-mad and the Nation of Islam. He worked for John Ali, who was the business manager for the Nation. John Ali introduced my father, William A. Woods, to the Honorable Elijah Muhammad. He recommended that the Nation of Islam do business with my father's accounting firm, Woods Accounting Service. We did their first whitefish-import deal for them. During this time I was basically the runner, when there were documents that had to be signed. I'm sure there were courier services back then, but small black businesses weren't using them.

There were numerous occasions when I would bump into both Malcolm and Louis, the Honorable Louis Farrakhan. Outside of the Honorable Elijah Muhammad's office, there was a long bench where people would wait to see him. On more than a few occasions, I would come tearing down the hallway with papers that the Honorable Elijah Muhammad needed to sign and I would be zoomed right past Malcolm and Louis Farrakhan sitting there waiting to converse with him.

Betty found this fascinating because she had not met my father, but she knew of him and his work with the Nation. She knew that he had passed and the whole story of how the Nation had been so supportive of handling his arrangements. That kind of started a different level of conversation between Dr. Shabazz and myself.

I told her about these events at our first meeting. I was so nervous, because I thought that I had insulted her. Betty had a very quiet sternness about her. As I said, she quietly reprimanded me for not following up and calling her, so I tried to tell her everything I thought would endear me to her. Plus, when you're talking to someone with the stature of Dr. Betty Shabazz—number one, I didn't believe I'd have that opportunity to begin with, and then, when I got it, I tried to tell her everything I knew in case I didn't get another opportunity. So I was talking fast and long.

After that initial phone conversation, she would always make me feel so special when I would see her at a fund-raiser, social event, the Urban League dinner, various functions. One of the things that I really admired about her was that she seemed to be able to get to so many places of importance to African American people. I could be in San Francisco at the NAACP's annual dinner, and, sure enough, there would be Dr. Shabazz. She and Dick Gregory just seem to have had a natural talent for being at African American functions of purpose and significance. I've always admired that in her, because it makes people feel really, really worthy and special when someone of importance will travel across country. And I'm sure she wasn't at all those functions she attended because somebody was her friend. I'm certain that a lot of those were just ones of many thousands of invitations she would receive, and she said, "Hey this looks like something I ought to lend my support to." She was like a one-woman cheering squad for black America.

No matter where I was, I would always approach her, and even if she was talking to someone, she would always refer to me by name. She would always make it appear to those around her that she knew me well personally. She'd always say, "Well, Cathy, I didn't know you were coming here," as if she and I had talked about it and I hadn't told her. And people would always say to me, "I didn't know you and Dr. Shabazz were friends—how do you know Betty Shabazz?" The way she would approach me made my presence seem a lot more significant to those individuals observing. Betty would say, "Oh, Cathy, we should have ridden out here together on the airplane," and people standing around would be like, *Wow.*

I really understand that, and now I try to do it. One of the things I'm sorry I didn't get the chance to do before she died was thank her for showing me, by example, how to encourage young people, because I do that now. When young people come up to me, I'll say, "How have you been? Did you finish that paper? Have you graduated from school yet?" I'm certain, within their circle, that they have the same reaction that I had with Dr. Shabazz, when people say to them, "I didn't know you knew Ms. Hughes." It makes that young person feel encouraged. It makes that young person feel special. I started believing the hype myself because there were numerous occasions where I felt comfortable just picking up the phone calling Dr. Shabazz, saying we were having something at Howard or we are doing X, Y, and Z, was she going to be in the area, could she come down? Oftentimes, it was something she was planning to attend anyway, or she would say, "No, I'm not going to be able to." Never, ever did I feel that she felt put upon when I called her. That's a very special quality when young ladies, young men are able to approach you, able to have conversations with you when in reality you really don't know them.

I have never been to Betty Shabazz's home, she had never been to mine, but I considered her a friend and I would hope she considered me one. Because that was the type of personality she had—she embraced you, she made you feel comfortable. She would always listen patiently. She might call up and ask me about something, and it might be one of those days where my son and I weren't seeing eye to eye on a particular problem and she would render advice. She reminded me of all the women that I really look up to. She was more African, to me, than the other older women whose advice and counsel I have sought. She was like the Queen Mother. Her advice was always so sound. She gave it in such a gentle, loving way. She didn't offer it like you had to take it. She offered it more as a matter of fact, the way some people can do, giving you advice almost like a psychiatrist gives you advice. It's not really advice, it's trying to stimulate you to make your own decisions. Well, Betty offered her advice like, "This is how I see it." In African cultures, parents rule supreme, they are adult-based societies. Even though you may reach adulthood, if your parents are still alive, you are still considered their child. And that's very much how I saw her, complete with the situation with her taking the grandson in, that's very African. When the children have trouble, it is the elders who step in to correct whatever the problem or situation is.

I remember saying to her that Malcolm could not have picked a better person to be the mother of his children and that he had to be very, very proud of what she not only had done with her life but what she had done with his children and his memory. She said that when you are picking a mate, you never know until the end result. She's the one who told me that in rearing children, you never know until that child goes to their grave whether or not you have been successful. I was telling her that she should be really proud, and she said that one of the mistakes that parents make is that they see success as an end as opposed to a process. None of us really know whether or not our lives have really been successful until the life is over. I thought that really fascinating.

The last conversation we had was in February 1997, at the Trumpet Awards in Atlanta, Georgia. She and Mrs. King were there together. I introduced her to Jeff Majors, and she shared with me that she, Coretta, and Myrlie Evers were all planning to take a cruise. I spoke with her three or four times, because she literally had me in stitches. She was teasing me about robbing the cradle, because Jeff looks about fifteen to twenty years younger than he actually is. When I came back over the second time, without him, her first question was, "How old is he?" I told her that he was in his forties, and she said, "Are you sure? Coretta and I could have sworn we smelled pabulum." I sat down and they started teasing me like we were teenage girls. Every time I stopped by her table, she would make these clever little remarks. Jeff probably had the greatest evening of his life because he just couldn't believe that the great Coretta Scott King and the great Dr. Betty Shabazz were sitting across the room talking about us. I mean, Betty was really giving me a rough time. I felt like I was a contemporary—I no longer felt like a young girl seeking her approval or attention.

This was shortly before she passed. I felt that her goodness was showing all the way to the end. She was trying to save her grandson all the way to the end. After I learned how severely she was burned, I started asking God to allow her to go in peace. I really didn't want to have her go through that, I did not want to ever see her have to struggle again. Her life had been one continuous struggle, here she has six daughters, her husband assassinated in front of her, and she was able to overcome all of that. I thought her trying to fight back physically from this fire as being an unfair challenge at that stage in her life. It's not a graceful exit. She deserved a graceful exit because she was a graceful woman.

Betty was so very African. Betty Shabazz reminded me of my Grandma, who kept money in her brassiere. One of the things that I was not surprised to learn after the injury to her was the reason that she wanted her pocketbook out of that apartment: She had several thousand dollars in that pocketbook. Individuals who knew her a lot better than me told me that she always had lots of cash on her. That just fit very consistently with my image of her being that old-fashioned African woman, who never knew when she might need a couple grand to bail somebody out of trouble, to hit the road, or whatever. There's this notion that old black women kept their money tied up in their handkerchiefs, their brassieres, or in their girdles back then because they didn't trust banks. Most of those women also had bank accounts, but there was a certain mentality in our culture of women as the protectors—women felt they always had to keep a few hundred dollars crumpled up in there because they never knew what emergency might come up. A rainy day is what my grandmother used to call it. Betty Shabazz had more than her share of rainy days.

Betty's hairstyle was the only thing I felt was inconsistent, but, then again, when a tragedy befalls someone like that and you are praying for them, you have a lot of time to think about them and things that you don't normally think about. One day when I was thinking about her, I wondered if she didn't have arrested development about her hair. Right up to the day she passed, she wore the same hairstyle she wore in her glory days with Malcolm, and I wondered if that was maybe her way of holding on to a piece of the past and if she had not really grown past that point. That there was a part of her emotions that were frozen back to those days. When I met her, she was the widow of Malcolm X, she had gotten her Ph.D., and I knew that she had successfully reared her six children by herself. I knew that she was a woman of serious purpose. She had an aura about her, even more so, to me, than Coretta Scott King did, and maybe it's because Coretta Scott King had more visibility in the media. She wasn't as much of an enigma—Coretta Scott King didn't have the mystique to me that Betty Shabazz did.

[
B E T H A N N　H A R D I S O N *is the president of Bethann Management, a talent agency in New York City. Her clients include actor Kadeem Hardison and model Tyson Beckford.*
]

A s a child I didn't know Betty, but I knew she was married to Malcolm. My father, Ameer Hassan, was a well-known leader in the Islamic community, an imam. In the 1950s, Elijah Muhammad, who had established himself in Chicago and was growing in power, had summoned my father to Chicago to meet with him. Elijah talked about what they were trying to accomplish. The second time my father went to see Elijah, he met Malcolm.

Because of my father's position in the community, the Nation (Elijah Muhammad Muslims) wanted to get support from him before coming to New York. My father had to admit that as much as he admired what Elijah had accomplished, the Nation still was not, as far as he was concerned, practicing religion. The nation was more about culture than it was about religion. They—the Nation—were able to take an enormous number of black men and turn them around and begin to give them a certain amount of unity and respect. That grew greatly. So, culturally, things were successful in one sense. But it was a difficult time. The Nation was trying to build "one people" while neutralizing the other. When they spoke to the black race about social issues, economics, politics, it was in support of the black race. In order to do that successfully you have to indicate and show just cause—or look toward the oppressor, which at that time was the white man. Of course it comes across like they are preaching hate. But that was not their intention because in the eyes of Allah (God), every man is equal. The point was economical and social issues.

I had met Malcolm when I was a child, about thirteen. Elijah had begun to really take a stronghold in New York because he had someone like Malcolm to lead that particular mosque. Malcolm was able to be an independently powered, speaking representation of the Muslims—the Elijah Muhammad Muslims I should say, because the sect makes a great difference. Malcolm eventually wanted to go to Mecca, which is the holy city of Islam, in the Middle East. My father was asked if he could make some sort of arrangement or make it easier for Malcolm to go. He had applied for a visa before and had been rejected. My father explained to Malcolm that it would be quite difficult — that he probably would never get the opportunity to go. They wouldn't accept him to come in, because of the way that the Nation was known and what they spoke of and how they preached. Eventually, as time went on, Malcolm began to see a different light and embraced traditional Islam. That's when the problems began.

Malcolm stayed close to my father at that time. He wanted to go to Mecca. He had grown and — in a way — softened. Eventually, he was able to enter the city of Mecca, and he became more of a religious Muslim rather than a radical Muslim. That was when everything changed and that was when his life ended. My father stayed close to him then, because Malcolm had taken a different stance and needed a great deal of support. I don't think Malcolm thought he was going to be killed. If he had thought he was, it was just accepted doom. It wasn't something I could imagine was a worry, but I have no idea of that, so it would be unfair for me to make that statement.

What I learned after Malcolm's death was that my father had organized the men — Muslim men — to pick up the body and make sure that Malcolm was buried within twenty-four hours. In the teachings of Islam, you have to be buried within twenty-four hours, a custom similar to Judaism. Only later did I also learn that my father had the strength to go and have him buried despite the fact that people were threatened and told no one should touch Malcolm. The word was out to leave Malcolm. But my father called a few men and told them, "There is no way we can leave this brother there, we have to go and get him." In the Islamic religion you have to be cleansed, you have to be dressed in a shroud, and you have to be properly prepared when you pass away.

♗

I got to know Sister Shabazz during the long period after the death of Malcolm. I'm sure I met her as a little girl, but the first time I met Betty as an adult was at a book-release party for a book on the black woman in America. She brought all her daughters. Prior to that I had known Attallah, and how she searched me out is a very interesting thing because of the relationship my father had with her father, and how important my father was to Malcolm, which people wouldn't have known about.

I didn't tell Betty of my knowledge of the relationship between my father and Malcolm until much later. Of course, I had met the girls; they were all grown up at the time. The girls had grown up, and each of them had searched me out for different reasons, with different needs to develop certain things they wanted to do in their lives. I always kept in my mind the knowledge and support my father had given Malcolm, my father telling him at that time that he was so radical and as long as he preached the way he did, that he would never be able to enter Mecca. In his own arrogance Malcolm thought that was quite untrue. But as far away as Mecca is, they know everything that's happening here. So at the time he wasn't able to go, but eventually, when he began to embrace traditional Islam, his mentality changed. That's when he became not as important to the Nation community.

When I eventually told Betty of the relationship my father had with

Malcolm, she tried to remember my father. She was like, "Ameer Hassan, of course?" It threw her off because she's looking at his daughter and thinking back in time to who he was and how things were.

Betty was a wonderful accomplishment, in a sense, because she had continued to master herself, her education, and she raised the children. I always asked how the girls were, and she'd always say, "I don't know. You know how it is, I'm like a mother who basically lived in a shoe and so many children she didn't know what to do." Like she was saying that you couldn't keep up with them. We both attended the Women's Leadership forum in Washington, D.C. It's funny that all through my life, my adult years, she was there. So I was always in touch with her. I always had some reason — if she was at a place or an event I was attending, we always had that communication.

My relationship with Betty was something I knew quietly. I knew the relationship with my family — my father to her husband. I always kept it in my head. She remembered my father; it was something we shared. It was a smile. It was always a little something more, that you had with someone as you lived amongst many that you know. It was more of a quiet acknowledgment.

It seems like the women who are icons for black women in America—Dr. Tucker, Dr. Height, Rev. Barrow, and Ms. Evers-Williams—were the women who were most forthcoming about Betty Shabazz. They understand history and the purpose of making it and passing it on. This is something that we've neglected to do since the sixties. This is where the huge gap came between our younger and older generations.

Dr. Height was funny, because even though she had given me a time to call, she was a little bit absent when I did—she was watching a football game! She wanted me to call her back. Dr. Height's a football fan, and it was the play-offs. It was refreshing to see these women as human beings, as girlfriends, because our generation doesn't see them that way. I hope I'm bridging the gap between the young and old; Dr. Betty always said not to forget the children.

Educating and uplifting other people was very important to Betty, and she did that by working at Medgar Evers College and through her radio show on WLIB. So I had to include two of the women that she worked with in the last few years of her life—Safiya Bendele and Cynthia Smith—as well as her old friends and colleagues.

DR. C. DELORES TUCKER *is convening founder and current chair of the National Political Congress of Black Women and president and founder of the Bethune Dubois Institute, both headquartered in Washington, D.C., and former secretary of state of the Commonwealth of Pennsylvania.*

THE late Betty Shabazz that I knew as a friend and loved was a royal icon of womanhood, motherhood, and sisterhood. When we honored her along with Myrlie Evers-Williams and Coretta Scott King at the annual brunch of the National Political Congress of Black Women in September of 1996, it occurred to me that all three "M" widows (of Malcolm, Medgar, and Martin) were truly ICONS of strength, love, and long suffering. Betty was the only one with six children, two of whom she was carrying in her womb, at the time her husband was brutally murdered before her very eyes. From that day until the day of her death, she was the quintessential personification of motherhood and womanhood.

Her living and dying set standards of sharing, caring, and love that few of us could ever hope to achieve. Her life taught us so many lessons. She demonstrated that by sheer will and determination one could overcome any manner of adversity to pursue one's dreams and goals in life. She showed us this by returning to school after raising her family and obtaining her doctorate. Dr. Betty Shabazz epitomized the Renaissance women of this age. There were no bounds or barriers that could stop her from probing the frontiers of knowledge. She was always talking about some interesting book she had just read, some article she'd heard about, or a concept that she was hatching in her mind.

I first met Betty in 1971 just after becoming the first African American Secretary of the Commonwealth of Pennsylvania. Our bonding was instant. My admiration and appreciation for her and the symbol of courage and tenacity that was ingrained in her very presence was overwhelming. Her expressions of how proud she was of my accomplishments created a special bond of sisterhood. At that time Betty was busy raising her beautiful brood of six children and this did not allow her to move around the way she did in later years. She would always call me when she came to Philadelphia to visit her three brothers.

As Betty's family matured, her movements increased to the point where we were often encountering each other at some conference or convention where she and I would be speaking. This was always a time of stimulating discussion about current issues; then there would be small talk and sisterhood talk. These occasions were a source of deepening friendship.

Several years ago, Betty became a part of our Black Family Leadership Group led by the late Tom Skinner and his wife, Barbara Skinner. Betty's presence and participation, along with her deliberate orations, always stirred a sense of excitement and anticipation within the group.

Her charming smile, easy manner, and kindly spirit were not to be taken for granted by anyone, because she was a strong-willed person who demanded respect everywhere she went. After our morning sessions, we would always find time to go shopping after lunch. Betty loved to shop. The first thing she would always say to me was, "CD, where are we going shopping?" We shared many experiences and had great fun on our shopping sprees (other Family members who often joined us included Dr. Maya Angelou, the Reverend Willie Barrow, and the Honorable Constance Newman). Our only time of serious disagreement occurred at the cash register, when she would insist on paying for the items I had purchased and I would say, "No, I am paying for you." We always had to argue ourselves into a standoff. She was just all giving as a woman, friend, and mother.

There was always some unique dimension of Betty's personality revealing itself. I was unaware of the source of her strong faith and social activism until her adoptive mother died a few years ago in Detroit. I was privileged to be there with Rosa Parks and speak at her funeral, and Betty was extremely pleased that Mrs. Parks accompanied me. I found out that the faith and strength that Betty possessed had been inherited from an early age. Her mother was an activist long before the Civil Rights movement. She was organizing demonstrations and marching in front of stores back in the forties, when Betty was a little girl. Her constant message to people was that they should not patronize any store that did not respect their dignity and offer them opportunities for employment. While engaging in protest marches, she was also considered a leading pillar of her church. I said to Betty after the funeral, "I always thought that the source of your faith, dignity, strength, and commitment to justice for our people came from Malcolm." She said, "No girlfriend, I grew up with that ingrained deep in my soul. If anything, I inspired him."

The images of Betty's funeral are still very vivid in my mind. My husband and I attended the services at the Riverside Church and the Muslim Temple in New York. The scene at the church was emotionally riveting, with Myrlie and Coretta recounting the times they had spent with Betty on retreat trips sharing their unique experiences of the assassinations of their husbands. It was their voices and the sight of Betty's daughters standing before the overflowing throngs at the Riverside Church that brought the reality of her death full circle in my mind. At the Muslim Temple in New York, the finality of Betty's death was not realized by me. I kept thinking that Betty would stand up and begin to speak.

As with all funerals, the really traumatic eruptions occur at the gravesite, when the moment of pending finality overwhelms you. When this recognition of eternity seized upon my soul, I could not contain the tears that had welled up in my eyes. Cicely Tyson and I were standing together and as they lowered Betty's remains into Mother Earth, we both broke into uncontrollable sobbing. As we did this, I cried out to Betty and promised her that I would always strive to complete her work that she left undone. I asked Cicely to join with me and proclaim to Betty that we would carry on her work. We stood there and we just couldn't stop crying, even though I knew she was better off than all of us. Why? She was going home to be reunited with Malcolm and her mother. Later, when the burial service was over, I committed myself to being available for the girls, to continue where she left off, because they were always at the heart of her concerns. I told the girls that I had made a commitment to their mother, to be there for them when they needed me. I lingered at the gravesite after everyone had left, gazing upward and downward, trying to find an answer to explain her eternal absence from our earthly presence.

I took a flower and planted it in the soft earth that covered her remains. I could not help but think of what a tremendous loss the family, the nation, and the world had suffered. I thought of how much her gifts of understanding, compassion, hope, and love were needed. Her family needed her so badly because she was the glue that held them together in times of unimaginable turmoil and grief.

After thinking about the loneliness and grief of the girls, we invited them to our Black Family Leadership retreat in Boca Raton, Florida. We all felt that the girls needed to be embraced in our circle of healing, our circle of bonding, and our circle of love. When it was time to depart, they all said what a soulful and spiritually energizing experience it had been. We look forward with joy to their presence at our next retreat when we will be joined by the newest member of the Shabazz family, Malikah's daughter, Betty Bahiayah Shabazz, named after her grandmother, Betty Shabazz.

Sister Betty frequently reiterated a saying of her dear mother which stated, "You have to find the good and praise it." Well, Sister Betty, your very presence epitomized and illuminated good and for that . . . *WE PRAISE YOU! WE PRAISE YOU! WE PRAISE YOU!*

D R . D O R O T H Y H E I G H T *was the president of the National Council of Negro Women from 1957 to 1998. She is currently chair and president emerita.*

I met Betty shortly after Malcolm's assassination. A friend of mine, Ellis Haizlip, who then was at Channel 13, thought we should meet, and he was right. She had had a rough time. Ellis made it a point to introduce us—she came into the city and he just made sure that we found a way. Needless to say, I was pleased to meet her and, like everyone else, I was sharing the sense of loss. But I must say she showed a great deal of courage and bravery. She was really one of the most generous and interesting persons I knew. She had such a great sense of humor. We had a relationship in which she would see something that she thought I liked, or I admired something she wore, and the next thing I knew, I had one.

I remember that she was one who would make her calls anytime, but particularly early in the morning. We had been together at all of the United Nations Women's Conferences, except I didn't go to Beijing. So one morning, very early, I got this call from her from Beijing, just to say, "Well, I wish you were here," nothing in particular. That was the kind of person she was. She was thoughtful. I liked the fact that she worked with me on so many things. She chaired the NCNW convention when it was in New York. It was her idea that we should be on a billboard. She made all the arrangements, and we had a billboard, "Welcome to New York," that could be seen from the Triboro Bridge. I had never seen that before at any of our conventions. She was in all of the Black Family Reunion celebrations, and was one of the most popular speakers because she shared so many experiences. I always remember her talking about her children. She told of having a housekeeper she kept because her children liked her and what that meant to her. She often came home from work and had to do all the work that she had paid the housekeeper to do. She said that one time, she just sat down and said, "Oh, this is too much. I'm tired of being the mommy," and one of the children said, "Well, let me be the mommy." And Betty went on to tell how, from then on, they shared together. The girls shared the responsibility with her.

Betty was a great friend and I loved her. We would talk about health issues and we usually came out on the same side. She was just a beautiful person.

I first heard about her death on the television. I was, like everyone else, distressed and saddened, because she was such a caring person. I thought it was like her to fight to the end. She was more concerned about her friends than about herself.

The thing that stands out for me is what fun it was to be around, to talk with and to travel with her. We traveled to Taiwan together and I teased her about how we all are great shoppers. She was able to come back and say, "You have to bear in mind that I have six people, not just one," referring to the six children for whom she had to bring back gifts.

❧

I can never forget the time when the United Civil Rights Leadership was called to come to Pleasantville, New York, by Ossie Davis, Ruby Dee, and Sidney Poitier shortly after Malcolm X returned from Mecca. Malcolm wanted to talk and he asked them to bring us all together. He explained that too much effort was put on dealing with white prejudice, and he thought that much more attention needed to be put on black unity and on our learning to work together. I think all of us agreed that we would not allow the press to continue dividing us with its generalizations and misconceptions. He also had a new vision after his visit to Mecca; that's what he wanted to share.

Betty and I had a kind of special bond, because I think Betty recognized for too long that people were not up to date on Malcolm. She heard so many interpretations that were just way off. Some were romantic and some were just plain inaccurate. It was always a pleasure to talk with her about him. She appreciated the opportunity to talk to someone who had some sense of him and who he really was, especially in his later days.

Of the meeting, I remember that Lorraine Hansberry was lying on a couch when Malcolm said that we needed to talk to each other and not about each other through the press. She leaned up and said, "Well, Malcolm, I agree with you, but how do you think I felt lying in a hospital fighting for my life and I heard you say I was disloyal to my race because I married a white man? You didn't ask me who he was or what I knew about him or why I married him." And Malcolm just said, very gently, "You're perfectly right, sister." And that was all he said. His humanity came through quite clear! So when I was talking with Betty, she said, "Well, that's a side of him that often was not known." She told me about one of the younger children. Wherever Malcolm was, when he came in, he always had oatmeal cookies and milk with her. After he was assassinated, it was a long time before she was able to get over just wondering where he was—wondering whether he was going to come and have cookies. People never saw that human side of him. That gentility.

ℬ

B E T T Y and I shared many, many good times together. We went to different events together, we traveled together. She was a wonderful dancer. She taught me the electric slide. She promised to teach me the macarena. She knew all of that. I think of her as I would think of a sister, because that was the way that we related to one another. At times she would tell me things, but she didn't share why. She was always fun. I think that she was a tremendous role model. We cannot think of her in terms of tragedy; you have to think of her in terms of triumph, because she really took hold and made a strong life for herself. She made herself available to help others. She made herself one who was always ready to be of service. She was a very supportive woman.

Professionally, she accomplished a tremendous amount in a short period of time and under all kinds of conditions. I think that's why she became a private person — because she had goals and she wanted to achieve them. She wanted to make a better life for herself, her children, and her community. She was a person who had a real, basic self-esteem. I think she felt that she was loved by many, but I also think that she felt that there were many she couldn't trust. She was wisely cautious. She showed she was a supportive member in organizations. She was a favorite at the Black Family Reunion because she would sit and talk with people and not only answer questions but also share with them her thoughts. She saw the value, and it was never something that she was doing as a celebrity. She always did it as a person who cared about people.

[REPRESENTATIVE MAXINE WATERS *is a member of the United States House of Representatives.*]

I am sadly and slowly coming to the realization I will never again be able to pick up the telephone and call Betty trying to persuade her to respond to some organization's request to be their featured speaker. Nor will I ever again answer Betty's telephone call when she is attempting to assist some group with getting me to be their guest speaker.

I will never again see Betty at any of the Malcolm X celebrations where we met from time to time. I'll never see her again at the Congressional Black Caucus Foundation dinner in September and say to her, "Girl, you are looking great!" There will never be another time when we are seated on the same dais at one of the many celebrations, conferences, or conventions we attended together.

I will not have Betty's wise counsel on how to keep cool, nonconfrontational, and understated. And I will never lie to Betty again and say I'm going to be very cool, nonconfrontational, and understated.

We will never again be able to laugh at ourselves, our friends, and our families, reminiscing about all the silly things we observe and in which we participate.

I feel myself growing older and more tired. It's too much of a burden to love, respect, adore, and, suddenly—with no notice, no warning—lose someone.

With Betty's going home, part of me is going with her. There are too few good people, lovely people, kind people. Betty Shabazz was a good woman—solid as a rock—competent, capable, and self-confident. We all need to awaken each day with the assurance that there will be trees, rivers, mountains, air to breathe, food to eat, shelter, friends and loved ones. Today, I don't feel so sure about these things. Betty's death has shaken my very being.

Betty will be missed by all her children, her entire family, her hordes of friends and associates. I will miss her more than I can ever describe.

[
THE REVEREND WILLIE BARROW *is the chairman of the board of the Rainbow Coalition PUSH.*
]

I met Betty around the time that I first met Malcolm. I met her in Chicago, at a rally. Betty and Malcolm were a power couple. You hear a lot about power couples these days, but they managed together to accommodate and appreciate their own careers without compromising their marriage.

I like to describe Betty like this: She was a woman from the beginning. She was a wife second, she was a mother third, she was an educator fourth, she was a communicator fifth, and she was a mediator always. I think that Betty had all of those qualities, and I can't say they were hidden. I just think she knew how to work them out with a person like Malcolm, who was so public. He was written about in all the papers. She didn't let that overwhelm her. She was still that woman, that wife, that mother. She was still in that educating mode because she loved her children. She always talked about educating her children—but not only her children, young people also. She was known to love and to educate young people. That was all she talked about. She compared her girls to young people in her neighborhood where she lived and around the country.

There's another way I like to describe Betty: She loved systems. Systems, models, or pilots. That's why she could work in small settings. She could educate a group of girls. She could provide a process by which they could become educators, and that is what she worked toward. Even though after Malcolm's death she got her formal education, her real education, the common-sense education, the day-to-day education, she had all along.

We used to talk about being married, and she used to talk about the differences. She and Malcolm didn't always agree. They had their differences, but the differences really didn't matter a lot in their marriage. We used to laugh about it all the time, because we used to talk about the longevity of my marriage, and she used to talk about her's and Malcolm's. I told her, "Don't you let anybody believe that being married to one man all this long time, that we didn't have our mountains, our valleys, and our downs." She would always say, "You're going to do that. You're going to have your ups and your downs, especially if you can think, but you're not going to have many ups and downs if you can't think." She really saw herself as a thinker.

We talked about the stabilization of the family. She took pride in talking about how she was able to maintain and stabilize her family and to also have the line of communication that she had with Malcolm, no matter where he was. He would call and they would talk, and when he got home he was able to share some of the load. He could drop some of the stuff off on her and she was able to lug a lot of that because of her stability. I'm sure that everybody, especially when you live in front of the camera, needs somebody to bounce something off.

Betty was overwhelmed by Malcolm's death. . . . She had a lot to overcome. It was so horrible to lose her husband and the father of her children. She didn't talk about Malcolm's death, but she did talk about some of the people who nursed her back to life. I don't know their names, but I do know that they weren't all African Americans. She said,

"They came to my rescue and they worked with me and worked with me and worked with me and worked with me!" I mean, that was some time that they spent making sure that she survived.

She talked about getting married again, and there were a couple of men. I used to say, "Now, Betty, I think you and that fellow could get along," and she would say, "Girl, don't be telling me that." I said, "I think he would be just right for you." She'd say, "Now you know ain't nobody gonna marry me. I'm strong-willed. Ain't nobody going to marry me. I'm too hard to change." And we would just kind of laugh it off like that.

She was fun to be with, but only if she knew you. If she knew you, you could talk all night. And Betty loved to dance. She would get out there before anybody and start dancing. She liked to have a good time. We would go to dinner; she loved to eat. We all teased each other about dieting. She said, "Now, wait a minute, I have lost twenty pounds. Don't you see?" And not only that, she loved to shop. She, C. DeLores Tucker, and I. We used to be the ones that loved to go shopping when the leadership group got together. I used to tell her, "Betty, you've got to get out of those black dresses." We'd go shopping and I'd say, "Betty, we're not going to buy no black dress today—because Betty used to love black dresses. Not just for evening either. I would say, "The work that we do, the life that we live; girl, we got to wear colors. That's why I wear yellow, red, and green—because you've got to get an upbeat somewhere to get out here in these streets. Girl, you can't keep on wearing black, because death is too close to us. We've got to brighten the corners of life and give light."

23

WHEN I think of Betty's death, I think about the pain of the Kennedy family. I look there, and I can look at the pain and have some measurement of what they are going through. I think you just don't know — and sometimes you want to question God as to why some families just have so much pain and so much sorrow. I know she lost Malcolm and in the end she had to struggle alone. In the struggle and in the pain there aren't too many that would have gone back and gotten their degree. That woman worked hard, but she didn't like to brag. She was one of those molders and builders who worked behind the scenes, and I think that's why she's so missed. Most of us knew how committed she was. That Sunday morning, when I heard about her death, I was just crushed. I remember that Betty used to always say, "Girl, don't always be talking about these sects and orders. Yeah, I'm a Muslim and you're Church of God, but I'm going to the same place you're going." We never did make much of a wide difference between Islam and my religion.

> NIARA SUDARKASA *is the president of Lincoln University. The following is a speech she gave November 21, 1997, paying tribute to Dr. Betty Shabazz and thanking Black Entertainment Television and* Emerge *magazine for the establishment of the Dr. Betty Shabazz Endowed Scholarship Fund.*

WHAT an honor it is for me to participate in the King Center's special tribute to our late sister, leader, and friend, Dr. Betty Shabazz.

She was a highly respected educator, an unwavering supporter of historically black colleges and universities, an activist in her local community, and a leader in the national African American community. For those accomplishments alone, the King Center and this audience could honor her this evening. But we also salute Dr. Betty Shabazz as the long-suffering widow of El Hajj Malik El Shabazz, known all over the world as Malcolm X. His organizational mantle she left to others, but his essential mission she made her own. In the decades after her husband's assassination, she became a tireless traveler and resolute voice on behalf of economic, political, and social justice for the dispossessed and downtrodden from the South Bronx to Soweto. Yes, in her own way, in her own distinctive voice, and with her own disarming demeanor, she made the essential mission of Malcolm X her own. For that, too, we honor Dr. Betty Shabazz.

For her humanitarian efforts, we also pay tribute to Dr. Betty Shabazz. These have yet to be adequately documented and appreciated. She spoke out and lent her name to humanitarian and philanthropic projects undertaken by local and national service organizations, such as the National Council of Negro Women and Delta Sigma Theta, Inc.; civil rights groups, such as the NAACP; women's groups, such as the National Political Congress of Black Women and the Democratic Women's Leadership Forum; and educational institutions, including various historically black colleges and universities. We at Lincoln showed our appreciation of her by awarding her an honorary doctorate in 1995 and electing her a trustee in 1997, a few months before her death.

Not only did Betty lend her name to many philanthropic projects but without fanfare and with little or no public acknowledgment, she gave generously of her own modest resources in support of many such projects. Her support extended to international as well as national causes. I remember, for example, that on Nelson Mandela's second visit to the United States, before he became president of South Africa, a full house gathered to greet him at Metropolitan Baptist Church in Washington, D.C. When the Reverend Jesse Jackson made his appeal for contributions to the ANC's many human-rights initiatives in South Africa, Dr. Betty Shabazz, seated on the rostrum, was one of the first to make a donation in the thousands of dollars. For her generosity and humane instincts, we appreciate and applaud Betty Shabazz.

Then, many of us cherish and honor her because she was a member of our extended family and our friend. As I said at the national memorial service for Betty Shabazz, we loved her for many reasons, not the least of which was her remarkable ability to make us all feel special. Surely, she must have developed that wonderful, expansive, inclusive quality while bringing up her six daughters. When she spoke to me about them, it was clear that each one was special and each one received her own measure of love, attention, and respect. Betty extended this same quality to all her friends, and to all those she touched through her words and deeds.

[
JOHNNETTA COLE *is president emerita of
Spelman College. In the fall of 1998, she will join the
faculty of Emory University as Presidential Distinguished
Professor of Anthropology, Women's Studies, and
African American Studies.*
]

I miss our sister Dr. Betty Shabazz. I miss watching her light up a room at some function or other, moving from table to table, making everyone she touches feel better because she passed their way. I miss the countless references to Betty Shabazz and her good work that came whenever I was in a circle of our mutual colleagues and friends. Whenever I read something about our brother Malcolm, or heard his name called, I would always think of our sister Betty Shabazz as a living heroine, carrying on in her own way the struggle he waged. I miss being able to think of her as still living physically among us.

On those occasions when I was able to talk one on one with Sister Betty Shabazz, it was easy for us to find some common ground in our respect for the power of education. She believed as passionately as I do that education can not only transform the life of an individual but it can also lift up and ultimately free a people. As a Mississippi slave owner said in 1832, "knowledge and slavery are incompatible."

Betty Shabazz so believed in education that at an older age she engaged in the demanding academic work that led to her earning a doctorate. There is a lesson here for all of us. It is that basic lesson that it is never too late to return to the classroom. It is that fundamental axiom that with faith, tenacity, and a mighty lot of hard work, any of us can do amazing things.

Our sister Dr. Betty Shabazz also believed, and put into practice her belief, in the responsibility of each of us to do whatever we can to strengthen our communities and move our people forward. At Medgar Evers College, where she was deeply engaged in the sacred task of education, she would spend countless hours helping individual students — counseling a young brother who couldn't find his path; encouraging a mother who had returned to school to stay the course. And her many associations with civic, religious, and community organizations reflected her conviction that each of us must be our sister's and brother's keeper.

Dr. Betty Shabazz believed in us womenfolks. Surely, raising six daughters had given her endless evidence that women can and must hold up half the sky. And she had but to touch her own strength, her own intellect, and her own ability to make do when don't wanted to prevail, and she would experience women power.

I will continue to miss our sisterfriend, our woman of power, our beloved teacher and doer, our shero, Dr. Betty Shabazz. But with gratitude for all of her good work and inspired by the enormity of her courage, let me not only miss her but let us all honor her by staying in the struggle.

Betty Shabazz was never one to step out front and leave her sisters and friends behind. Of course, because of who she was, many of us who called her "sister" would have been content to walk in her shadow. But Betty was so magnanimous in gesture and generous in spirit that she would always deftly move aside so that those of us with her could share the spotlight that was focused on her. Because she taught us the true meaning and measure of sisterhood, we love and cherish the memory of Dr. Betty Shabazz.

I am honored to have been a personal friend of hers. In the months since she left us, I have missed our late-night and early-morning telephone calls, our shared confidences, her wise counsel, and her surprise visits. C. DeLores Tucker and I always tell the story of the time that Betty took a taxi from Harrisburg, Pennsylvania, to Lincoln University, over sixty miles through what might be called the backcountry, to be present for a Lincoln University convocation honoring C. DeLores. Betty paid me a number of such surprise visits, both at Lincoln and in Florida, where my husband and I often spend Christmas. Like many of her other friends, I also miss our special shopping sprees — but we won't talk about that here. There are so many things that I miss about Betty, but, fortunately, I have no reason to miss her spirit, because it is always with me.

> K A T H Y   J O R D A N   S H A R P T O N *is the wife of the Reverend Al Sharpton.*

D R . Betty Shabazz was one of my mentors. Whenever I needed to talk to someone, she was there to listen, learn, and give her opinion — which was not necessarily to be taken for advice. When I needed to know of a school where I could send my two daughters, Dominique and Ashley, who were her godchildren, she directed me. Just before she died, we were discussing the next level of education for them. The girls called her Auntie Betty. Some of our favorite times were spent at Wells, in Harlem, over fried chicken and waffles, where we talked, laughed, and cried for hours. Dr. Betty Shabazz will forever be in my heart, and all of the knowledge I've learned from her will be passed on.

One of her last appearances was as guest speaker at my birthday celebration on May 15, 1997, at the Canaan Baptist Church of Christ, where the Reverend Wyatt Tee Walker is the senior pastor, my church, where my family, friends, the National Action Network, and a committee of women from all walks of life saluted me. Well, Dr. Betty was there in all her splendor, as she paid tribute to me. I was so honored, I could not believe this giant of a woman, my mentor, was actually there for me. She had a great time, too; she really got a kick out of her godchildren and their father, the Reverend Al Sharpton, singing "I Believe I Can Fly." She really laughed when the reverend sang off key.

She said that if your husband, family, friends, and peers can publicly pay respect to you, then you are loved in a special way. Then she also said that she loved me!!! Every time my children and I pass the Medgar Evers College in Brooklyn, where we often visited her, we think of her. God bless the soul of our beloved Dr. Betty Shabazz. Truly, we respect her legendary husband, Brother Malcolm X, but her picture was hung in our living room first, because Dr. Betty Shabazz has always been there for my beloved husband, her godchildren, and me. I miss her very much.

[SAFIYA BANDELE *is the director of the Medgar Evers College Center for Women's Development.*]

DR. Betty Shabazz gave her last formal speech at our beloved Medgar Evers College on Saturday, May 24, 1997, at an event combining a career-development seminar with the Center for Women's Development's "Prayer Breakfast for African American Women Survivors of Childhood Physical and Sexual Abuse." Speaking movingly after hearing some of the women's stories, Dr. Shabazz said, "I remember growing up in Bethel AME Church in Detroit and having to remember Bible verses. I remember John 3:17: 'For God sent not His son into the world to condemn the world; but that the world through him might be saved.' " She said, "Therein lies our challenge and task. Changing the world by changing ourselves—that's a revolutionary task that all of us should be about." She told the "survivors" how important it was for them to know themselves and to organize their lives in a clear and focused manner. As a friend of the Center for Women's Development, Dr. Shabazz always recommended it as a place to assist women in this organization of their lives.

Dr. Shabazz's message on that date—less than a month before her death—contains these lessons for us, the living.

1. *Sisterhood is powerful.* For the twenty years that I've been at Medgar Evers College, she was my personal and professional advocate, and a strong supporter of the Center, where I've served as director since

1982. She would often interact with the women students who came for counseling, offering encouragement from recollections of her days as a young, struggling single mother having to learn who to trust. As she put it, "listen, predators come in all colors and guises." She believed in sisterhood in the best tradition of the historic Negro club women's movement; she joined and actively worked in women's organizations. On campus, she was a regular participant in Women's Center events. She was as passionate about the young Medgar Evers College student trying to earn her degree as she was about the women struggling to build income-generating projects in Uganda and Namibia.

2. *Change the world by changing ourselves.* Our continuing unwillingness to own up to and take responsibility for ourselves and our communities continues to hold us back. Changing ourselves means understanding the value and necessity of counseling for ourselves, our families, and our community. Changing ourselves means changing our hypocritical attitudes about single mothers and teen mothers; it means addressing the deep misogyny and homophobia in our communities. It means translating the rhetoric of "the children are our future" into action knowing that in reality the future is now. It's now for young Malcolm and the thousands of young Malcolms locked down in this country. If we don't act, we're collaborators in the escalating institutionalization of African American and Latino youth.

3. *Live by strategy.* Dr. Betty lived by strategy—having disparate friends and allies—moving in seemingly radically different circles be-

cause she understood the value of a certain kind of diversity. That she was "successful" was evident on June 24, 1997 (the date of her funeral): No woman of any color in recent U.S. history has brought together so many folks from all levels of government, education, the arts — and just folks.

The Center for Women's Development has lost a mighty friend and supporter. I have lost my sister, my godmother. The mother-daughter relationship between Dr. Shabazz and me was deep and satisfying. It was also challenging and reversible, as I would admonish her to take better care of herself, to limit her jet-setting, to look at things differently, and to allow her daughters to live their lives. Godmother, I will miss your regular questioning of my clothes — "God, Safiya, don't you have any clothes other than bright purple [or red or yellow]?" — to which I'd respond sassily, "I ain't gon' be monochromatic like you and wear navy blue and black all the time." Or she'd comment, "You know what you're wearing isn't matching," and I'd retort, "I ain't the matching kind." We would carry on like girlfriends, usually in her office, sometimes in my office. My own grandson is named Malcolm and she loved to hear what he was doing and saying. She had promised my son, Nwandu, a "little job" helping her at the college convocation on June 5 — but instead, she lay on that hospital bed dying. Godmother, I'll miss your late-night calls telling me about your adventures and some "idiot" or another. I'll miss jumping through hoops to get some report done for you, miss researching some aspect of women's history for your speeches, miss dashing to the store for your apple or carrot or broccoli juice, miss your "gifts" ("here, put this in your pocket, be careful . . ."). I promise to wear the eye concealer you gave me to hide the blackness under my eyes and to use that little blush stuff and brush. I will always smile remembering when your sisterfriend Coretta Scott King gave you a beautiful makeup bag to replace that Saran Wrap thing your thrifty self was using to hold your lipsticks—which you only recently began to wear. I will smile at your question, "You still seeing that guy?" referring to my beloved incarcerated fiancé, Ibn Kenyatta, and be thankful for your offer of material support in our fight to win his unconditional release. And I will smile at that low-down funky dance you did at my fiftieth birthday party.

People used to comment on our loving friendship, about how strange it seemed that we could be so close and be so different. We taught and learned from each other's difference. I was in your life to also—at this moment—remind the world that you were a flesh-and-blood black woman subject to everything y/our kind is subject to. You had your faults, like each of us: the good, the bad, the ugly.

Today, I remember your multidimensionality. As Alice Walker said about contradictions, you took them and wrapped them around your shoulders like a multicolored shawl.

And you kept stepping.

CYNTHIA SMITH *was program producer at WLIB Radio, where she worked on Dr. Betty Shabazz's radio program,* A Forum for Women. *Currently she is marketing director for the National Association of Black Owned Broadcasters (NABOB).*

PEOPLE come into our lives for reasons that sometimes do not immediately reveal themselves. I know why my path crossed with Dr. Betty Shabazz—she had a lesson to teach me. The lesson was on life. She gave me the opportunity to experience her love, humor, dedication, and strength. My tribute to her is to continue in the fight for humanity by making significant contributions and to continue on the road to personal achievement.

" 'Render unto Caesar what is Caesar's and unto God what is God's.' We have a number of agendas as human beings, particularly when we understand that our lives must be broadened and extended in order for us to function as full human beings."

Every Thursday for the past two years, Dr. Betty Shabazz opened her radio program, *A Forum for Women,* by reciting that passage. In the background played Chaka Khan's "I'm Every Woman." Her audience was loyal on WLIB 1190 AM, a New York City talk-radio station owned by family friend Percy Sutton.

I often watched in amazement as Dr. Shabazz danced and sang in her seat at the beginning of the show. You would sometimes hear her sing along—"I'm every woman . . . it's all in me." It was her theme song, and it fit her well. I must say that it was an honor to produce and work so closely with this icon. She commanded great attention without saying a word, and when she spoke, you listened. She gave the best advice and counsel because you knew it came from her heart—and her experiences. From the first day I met Dr. Shabazz I was overwhelmed by her presence. Who would believe that our paths would cross in such a way? That I would be so fortunate to work with a woman who quietly made history every day of her life? She used her celebrity status to turn the spotlight on others. That was her way.

Dr. Shabazz used her program to educate women and men on how to use resources available to them. She made sure that guests left the audience with issues to think about and critically examine. Her guests ranged from book authors, community activists, and everyday people to heads of state, celebrities, and business leaders. She discussed a variety of topics, including education, politics, health, and youth-oriented issues. It was her way of giving back to the community.

I have very fond memories of Dr. Shabazz: I will always remember the wonderful smell of her perfume and the jingling of her jewelry. If she happened to slip in without me seeing her, her scent and that jingle announced her presence. The way she liked her herbal teas, decaffeinated black coffee, and hot apple turnovers—when we were not watching our weight that week. Her love for watermelon.

During our last conversation, we laughed heartily about some of the things that actress Kim Coles, her guest that day, had written in her relationship book *I'm Free, But It'll Cost You.* We talked about the show's schedule for the following week, and concluded by saying we would talk on Friday because she was going out of town.

Before the end of her show that day, I secured her car service. Promos for the next show were lined up. I was on my way out the door to another business meeting when she said to me, "You're leaving me unattended, Cynthia?" "Of course not, Dr. Shabazz," I responded. "Everything is taken care of. I'll talk with you tomorrow." I did not know that May 29 would be my last interaction with a woman I so admired. She gave me inspiration, guidance, and strength. The news about Dr. Shabazz's accident put me in a state of shock. I was devastated. I rushed to Jacobi Hospital, only to feel helpless. There was nothing I could do but pray. And I did—for her and her family.

I am thankful to the most high that I on numerous occasions told her that I loved her. As I write this, I know she is overseeing every word. So, Dr. Shabazz, thank you for pushing me and for giving me advice on how to live my life to be an example both professionally and personally; for keeping me mindful of my responsibilities, my femaleness, and my blackness; for letting me walk, talk, and dine with you as heads of state entertained you. I miss your early-morning calls.

I treasure the time that we spent in our pajamas on a business trip in Washington, how we shared our beauty secrets, ate fruit, and watched CNN until you drifted off to sleep. How you fussed with me about my appearance on days when I looked like I felt. You are truly missed.

On Thursdays, I still look forward to seeing you come through my office door. When I hear "I'm Every Woman," I am rendered speechless. When days at work are overwhelming, I visit the production studio because it's there where I connect with you spiritually—it's there where I saw you last. You are a star continuing to shine brightly, reminding us that the struggle continues and that there is much work to be done. At the burial, I spotted in the crowd a friend from college. As I approached to say hello, one of the picture stands began to topple. I moved quickly to save the picture before it tumbled to the ground. It was a picture of Dr. Shabazz. I thought back to our last conversation when Dr. Shabazz asked if I was leaving her unattended. Upon catching the picture the question was answered again. No, I am not leaving you unattended. I am always going to have your back and you will always have my love.

One of the things that was revealed to me was that she cared about and took time for everybody. No matter who they were, she was not one of those people who are just cordial. She really followed up. She spent a lot of time nurturing her black children; she made a big impact on them. Betty looked after everyone's children. Betty nurtured; in my mind, she was an African mother, and black people were her village.

Moving through this, I'm wondering where she got the strength . . . where she found the time to make the sacrifice. I'm younger than Betty, and I wouldn't have the strength or energy to keep it all together like she did, seemingly effortlessly.

[IYANLA VANZANT *is one of Dr. Shabazz's former students at Medgar Evers College and the award-winning and bestselling author of* Acts of Faith, In the Meantime, *and* One Day My Soul Just Opened Up.]

I was babbling, going on and on, without taking a breath, trying to communicate the fact that I was in trouble. *"The meeting had run longer than I expected—two people had an altercation—one had thrown a chair at the other—I had had every intention of ordering the food earlier, but had forgotten in the process of getting ready for the meeting—the police had taken so long to come, and when they got there, they handcuffed the wrong person—this was all they needed and wanted to nail me—the guy who threw the chair was a nut! A real nut! There wasn't enough time to call anyone now! I was expecting at least thirty people and I had nothing for them to eat!"* Dr. Betty, which is what I called her, sat stark still, staring at me. Suddenly, without batting an eye, she sat forward in her chair, grabbed a pad, and began scribbling. I kept talking, I mean babbling. She turned the pad around, shoved it in my direction, and began to tap on it with her pointing finger. What she had written on the pad stopped me in midsentence: *What is it that you are trying to say? What is it that you need?*

Regardless of the reason, whenever I walked into her office, in need, in trouble, babbling, crying, or in rage, she rose to the occasion. But, that's what Betty Shabazz did best. She rose. She rose to the need at hand. She rose to whatever the responsibility or challenge facing her called for. She rose on behalf of those whom she loved. She rose to the causes she held dear. On that particular day, she rose high enough to come down to my level, pull me up to her level, and got me out of trouble. She called a caterer friend who delivered a three-course meal for my student council meeting within ninety minutes. The meal was fantastic. I was saved. Dr. Betty had done it again—worked her stuff, created a miracle, saved my butt, and taught me a powerful lesson: You have the resources to do whatever you need to do, whenever you need to do it.

When I first became a student at Medgar Evers College in Brooklyn, I thought Dr. Betty Shabazz was larger than life. In those days, before I got a chance to know her up close and personal, I didn't think of her as a real person. She was, after all, Malcolm's widow! She had been on television! And radio! She was a star! A real star! She, I thought, was more than I could ever hope to be. She had been through and overcome things I could not even imagine. Many times when I would see her walking along the corridors of the college, my heart would pound, my mouth would become dry, and I'd try not to stare at her. I can now admit that I would purposely turn my head in fear that if I saw her up close, something would happen. I'm not sure what I thought it was, but I wasn't taking any chances. I now realize that I did to her then what I resist being done to me now; I dehumanized her. In my own career, I have discovered that when you are viewed as strong and powerful, when people hold you in high esteem, those same people have a tendency to forget that you are a human being. Human beings have feelings. Human beings have challenges. Human beings have dealings with other human beings based on real human feelings, that result in real human challenges. In that respect, Dr. Betty Shabazz was no different from the rest of us. The one stark difference I came to see was that a lot of her *"human stuff"* was handled in public.

One day, she snuck up behind me. Well, not really. She was passing by as I was talking with a fellow student. Suddenly she turned to us saying, "What you got in there? It sure smells good, and I'm starving!" I stopped breathing. *"Oh My God! Betty Shabazz just talked to me! In public!!!!!"* I thought she was kidding. I thought that she would keep walking, and not see me fall to the floor, gasping for air. She didn't see me fall. She stopped and asked us again. "What you got to eat in there?" The other student, who was probably as awestruck as I, responded, "I don't have anything! She's got it! She's got the food!" O great! Put it on me! Knowing I can't breathe or speak. Put the responsibility for answering Dr. Betty Shabazz on me! In public!

"Chicken," I said. "It's chicken from the Chinese restaurant."

"Do you want to share? I'm starving. Your treat today. My treat tomorrow. Come on, I've got some plates and napkins."

And so began my blessing. The very private blessing of knowing Dr. Betty. My star. My surrogate mother figure. My sister, elder, friend, with whom I have shared many great meals, many long talks, and many moments away from public view.

On most occasions, the meals we shared were of little importance. I was blessed in that she fed my soul and my mind. She carefully watched as my career grew, always giving me helpful little tips about dealing with the public: "Put your mint in the tissue. That way you can get it in and out of your mouth inconspicuously." Making financial decisions: "Whatever you do, pay your taxes on time! Don't let the IRS need to look for you—ever!" And choices that would advance my work: "Make sure the people around you know who's in charge. Watch them, and remember who works for who!" She once called me at 2 A.M. to tell me about an idea she thought I should pursue. When I tried to explain to her that I had already tried what she was telling me, she responded, "Yes, but sometimes people don't stick with things long enough to give them time to grow." Once again, I was awestruck. I was so sleepy and in such awe that I couldn't get my mouth open. She could, and she did just long enough to say, "Goodnight," and hang up. I didn't sleep for the rest of the night. *"How dare she know what I needed to do—again! How dare she be so right about my willingness to give up so soon."* But, she knew. And, she was right—again! When I admitted that to myself, I tried exactly what she said. I started a newsletter. It worked, and it's still working, seven years later.

Once I really got to know her, I was no longer in awe. I was amazed! It was absolutely amazing how real she was. She was a real person, with real feelings, real concerns, and something real to say about it all. There were times when we had real girl conversations about life, and men, and each other. I came to know when she was sad, angry, upset, or troubled. Mind you, I didn't see any of this in her manner. Nor did I hear it in what she said, because Dr. Betty would never let on that anything was the least bit out of whack. However, something happens when you break bread with a person over a long period of time. You can feel what they feel. I believe that's how she knew what to do when I was in trouble. And, that's precisely how I knew what she was going through. Although we never talked about it, there were things we knew about each other, and I'm sure she prayed for me as hard as I prayed for her.

Once I graduated, the meals stopped, the frequency of the conversations lessened, and our relationship moved to another level. Several times when we were at public events together, Dr. Betty would introduce me as one of her "little students." At first I felt honored that she would admit that she knew me. As time went on, as I grew, as my career advanced, I didn't want to be a little student. I wanted her to be proud of me. I wanted her to acknowledge how far I had come. Just like a child vying for the mother's approval, I wanted her to give me my due. Of course, just like a child, I dared not challenge her. But as always, she knew. As life would have it, I was a speaker on a program, and Dr. Betty Shabazz was asked to introduce me. After her own standing ovation, she began to introduce me, admitting that she had trouble pronouncing my "new" first name, but she did it perfectly in public. She went on to say that I was one of her many "little" students who had gone on to do great things. Then, without warning, she corrected herself, in public. "She's all grown up now, so I guess I'd better stop calling her little." If I hadn't been in public, I would have cried. Mother, elder, sister, friend, Dr. Betty Shabazz was giving me my due! In the way she lived her life, gracefully, calmly, with great focus, and with a lot of love.

The last time we shared time together was not for a meal. It was at a public event in June 1997, in the amphitheater of Medgar Evers College, where I was the commencement speaker. We sat next to each other, the way we had in her office fifteen years earlier. She gave me a mint, in a tissue. She was always reinforcing the life lessons she taught. She asked about my children. She had watched them and me grow right there at the college, and although she could never remember their names, she cared enough to always ask about them. She told me that she loved my last book, and thought that it was very wise to dedicate it to Medgar Evers. Betty Shabazz calling something I had done wise! If we had not been in public, I would have cried—again. The college president awarded me the Presidential Medal of Honor for service to the community that day. Gently, Dr. Betty took the medal from around my neck, held it in her hands, and said she would have it framed for me. In her very busy human schedule, she never got around to doing it. After I spoke, she asked me about my mint. I showed her that I had put it back in my mouth, inconspicuously. Slowly, deliberately, in the way she always did when she was pleased, she shook her head in approval. I smiled to myself as the warm rush I felt moved throughout my body.

After all the degrees had been conferred while the college president was making his final remarks, Dr. Betty Shabazz, the very strong, very powerful public widow of El Hajj Malik El Shabazz, quietly, and in full view, put her hand on my knee. Without turning her head to draw public attention, she said to me, "You did very well. Yes, you did." Those were the last words she spoke to me, and they are the words and the way I will always remember her.

[A N A N D A L E W I S *is an MTV VJ.*]

I worked for Mayor Marion Barry's Youth Leadership Institute in Washington, D.C. Betty Shabazz was in Washington accepting a donation for herself and her daughters, and she accepted it in front of our kids at the ceremony. At least half our kids were there, at the ceremony. My kids were in there, and I was in there, and it was unbelievable. It was the first time I had seen her. When she spoke to the kids, I was looking at the audience from the back of the room, being an adult, a trainer keeping the room calm, and the kids were just enthralled with her. A lot of them barely knew who Malcolm X was.

They were enthralled with her as a person, and what it said to me was that her personality and her spirit were so pervasive that they broke through all the lack of knowledge. All of the "who *is* this woman" questions went away, because the heart of this woman was so clear to everyone. Looking at her, they knew that she loved people, she cared about kids, and she wanted to see this world become a better place than it is. And that's what they got, that's what they felt, and it wasn't even anything that she said.

She was telling the kids that despite all obstacles, stick with your dreams. She was telling the kids, do what it is that you think you're here to do and don't pay attention to any of the other stuff going on around you, because a lot of it is just someone trying to pull you off course. Because while you're on your course, you are in the light and you're doing what it is that you're supposed to do. Everybody doesn't want to see you do well, so you just have to keep your head in the grind and go for it; forget everything else. Be in the moment and use your time wisely. I think they gave her a standing ovation at the end. These are fourteen through seventeen year olds, and not that they are incapable of something like that, but things like ovations are drawn out of them only when it's somebody they know well and that they respect. And, like I said, a lot of them did not know the full story about who she was. But she came in there and blew their minds, and what I witnessed was the kind of person that she was—her strength was obvious, her ability to go on in life. She didn't completely break down after losing her husband and having all of these children to care for by herself.

But something more than her strength came across to me. She really loved people. She had experienced something that could have made her really bitter and angry towards the world. But it's like she could take her experience and turn it around and say, you know, nothing in life is guaranteed. Nothing is ever given to you with the understanding that you will have it forever. So just appreciate every single moment of every single day that you have with someone you love, so that when they leave you or if they're taken away from you, for whatever reason, you know that every step of the way you tried to make it the best that you could without much regret.

I cried. I cried all day, and what made it even harder was feeling that we need people fighting for goodness, light, and righteousness. Not even on a religious level, but just on a level of spirit that says we all innately know what is right and what is not. We know when it's good and we see the light, what it is, and people who are really tuned into that—we need more people like them in the world. I mean to tip the scale. The world, the global well-being, and the wealth, health, and prosperity of our people in this country and the country in the world is dependent upon how many people we have fighting for the light to shine. Because there are a lot of people trying to put it out. So to lose someone who was so in the fight, so for the cause of being bright, and shining her light on people and loving people and blessing people with her energy and spirit, for her to be killed like that was just horrifying to me. I still have a hard time dealing with it.

> RUTHIE THOMAS *founded Blackdolls Productions, a nonprofit organization that reaches out to youth through creative projects and programs.*

I wrote Dr. Shabazz a letter back in March 1997. At the time, I was a candidate for graduation at Fordham University, from an adult-education program in communication. Our group sat around and discussed who we would like as a keynote speaker. Our theme was moving forward with the millennium. Someone said, "How about if we try to get Dr. Shabazz?" People said, "We know we won't get her." But I said, "Let's try," and so it was put upon me to get in touch with her.

So I wrote her a letter at the school in Brooklyn where she was teaching, Medgar Evers College over on Bedford Avenue. When she called me back in a day or two, we talked about everything under the sun—except the graduation that was coming. She asked me a lot of questions about myself. How old was I? How did I feel about returning to school with a grown daughter? She wanted to know a lot about my plans, what my plans would be once graduating, and so forth. Then we talked about my home life; she asked me where I grew up, about my siblings, and so forth. She found that I had quite an unusual story, and we began talking about that. As the conversation moved on, we started to discuss the program for the graduation, which fell on May 10, 1997. She continued to call me as that date approached, and we talked back and forth. I said to her, "Dr. Shabazz, well, I'm going to be really busy that day, so how about if I have someone pick you up?" And she said, "No, no, you have to meet me because we've been talking for several days." And, of course, every time we talked, she found out a little bit more about me, how I took care of my grandmother, just little things like that.

Of course, at the graduation, she delivered a wonderful speech. When I met her—I don't know, I just felt in awe being in her presence. She was so warm to me, she told me to come and sit in the car with her and the driver, and she introduced me to him. We moved on into the school and did the ceremony and everything. I introduced her to people, and everyone was just taken by her presence. She wore a beautiful knit outfit, a dress with a sweater that went along with it, and she had her nice jewelry around her neck. I think she really appreciated large pieces of jewelry. We stepped into the ladies' room and she freshened up. I helped her into the Ph.D. robe—she didn't know that I went through hell and high water the day before to get the robe. I was so taken with talking with her almost every other day that I totally forgot to tell the faculty that we'd need a robe for Dr. Shabazz to speak in. How I remembered was Dr. Shabazz called me the day before the commencement and she said, "Ruthie, do you have a robe for me to put on?" And I lied—I said yes, knowing that we did not. I totally forgot and went through everything from left to right, but pulled it together. When she put that robe on on May 10 and looked in the mirror—you know how women do, they check themselves out—she said, "Oh, Ruthie, this is nice. Where did you get this?" I said, "Well, I got it from the president's office." But, I mean, I was on the phone with the secretary of Fordham University into the wee hours of the night because I didn't want to disappoint her. It was black and burgundy, and it was very sharp, too. She didn't care to wear the headpiece, though.

Her speech was about moving forward and keeping up with technology, reading and learning more about your history and other people's history, other cultures and races. After the speech was over, she said to me, "Ruthie, did I do a good job?" And I said, "Of course." I couldn't even believe she had to ask me that question. She gave a powerful, powerful speech. Again we talked and she gave me a mint, and when she gave me the mint she put me in mind of my grandmother, because you know the elders always kept a little mint in their purse or somewhere.

I had to give the opening speech presenting her. As I was giving the speech about how she was a pioneer and what she had done and been through and how she had seen history at its best and its worst, my eyes kind of shifted over to her. She was sitting over on my left-hand side, and I saw that her eyes were closed and she was shaking her head in agreement with what I was saying. She got a standing ovation.

After the graduation was over, she had me escort her back over to the car. I sat in the car with her and we talked. She asked me how I felt and I said good. She said to me, "We're going to keep in touch." Of course, sometimes you feel people say certain things like that just to be nice and you will never see them again. Four days after the graduation, though, she called me—it was 10:30 at night, and I had just laid down to go to sleep and the phone rang. She said, "This is Dr. Betty Shabazz." I was just taken again. And I said, "Well, Dr. Shabazz, is there anything I can do for you?" I really never expected that she would give me a call. Especially at 10:30 at night. She said, "No, nothing you can do. I was just calling to see how you were feeling and how you were doing since you graduated." I was almost teary-eyed. She told me, "Now that you have your graduate degree, walk carefully, continue to learn." That reminded me of my grandmother again.

It touched me so much that she continued to call me, and I felt blessed that she did. We had several other conversations. The last time Dr. Shabazz called me was actually May 23. She called me at 1:30 in the morning to say hello, and when she called I was, of course, knocked out.

We even talked about men a little bit. She said, "Girl, you know how they are, you know how they can be. You just have to look around them sometimes and look past them." And then she laughed. It was like a sister thing. We talked until about two. We talked about my life again; she encouraged me to write about my life and how I made it out of a home with drugs and incest and things like that. Having a daughter young, at age sixteen, and how I kept her and didn't throw her into the trash like some of these children are doing today. She met my daughter and she invited me to come to her home for dinner, but, unfortunately, that never happened. I knew that I was truly blessed because she had taken such an interest. Knowing that I had taken care of my grandmother, she asked a lot of questions about my mother. Where was she? Why was I the one taking care of my grandmother? She felt that if I told my story it might help someone else. It was funny, because I wanted to tell her that I had read so many stories about her and her children, and I had even collected pictures and magazines over the years. For some reason, I decided I didn't want to tell her that—I wanted her to know that I truly admired her, but I didn't want her to think I was a crazy person like that.

She talked about her six girls. She talked about being a single mother and raising her six girls. She said that it was definitely a struggle, and she said, "I know you are struggling with one, because I know it's not easy," times have changed. She had seen a lot of things in her lifetime that I in my lifetime was too young to know about. She said that she loved girls, little girls. I told her about when I was pregnant, and she asked me, "Well, did you want a girl?" I said, "Oh, yes. I prayed day and night for a girl." She said to me, "I have six wonderful daughters." She told me that she wanted me to meet one of her daughters. I don't know any of her daughters personally, but when she had mentioned inviting me over to dinner, she said, "I'd like you to meet one of my daughters, because I think she would really be interested in the program you just completed at Fordham University. When you come over, you'll meet her and you can explain what the program is, because I think it would be great for her." She never said which one. I was really looking forward to that.

Of the last few conversations we had, the last two or three were about me moving forward. She just advised me to carry myself in a certain way because I was a young lady. Oh, she told me too—and let me get this right—she said, "Don't tell too many people in corporate America what you are planning to do, because they will always stay two to three steps ahead of you." I remember that so well . . .

ℬ

I didn't go to the hospital because I figured I wouldn't get in. I mean, they don't even know who I am. That was very frustrating for me. That was frustrating because I had no proof—I had proof of who I am, but I had no proof saying that I'd just hung up the phone with this woman a week and a half ago. Not being a blood relative or a friend with any type of celebrity status, I felt they wouldn't let me in. What I did was I typed a letter to her oldest daughter, Attallah. Told her who I am and that I had just spoken with her mother and that we'd had several wonderful conversations, that we were going to have dinner, and such. I FedExed the letter to Attallah at the hospital, so that she would get it the next day, but not knowing whether or not she would get it directly in her hands because of what was happening. I put it to Attallah's attention. I pretty much figured that they would have someone at the hospital accepting mail, cards, and things like that. Maybe she got it, maybe she didn't, but I'm going on the notion that she did.

ॐ

M Y mom has been drug-free for about twenty-three years now. But my brother is now incarcerated. He had fought with drugs off and on, and this is a very talented young man. Smart children but the wrong guidance and things like that. I told Dr. Shabazz that my mother was not there for my graduation in grade school, nor was she there when I graduated with a master's. Having my daughter young at sixteen, I was forced to leave school, and I've always had a goal and a dream to finish. When I finished college in 1994, I never thought that I would go on and get a master's in anything, because my goal was just to finish college. That's one of the main things that I always wanted to do. And I know Dr. Shabazz would encourage me. So, I'm so grateful to have known her and I know I have lost a truly wonderful mentor. I can only think about the conversations we would have had.

*When I called Laura Ross Brown and she told me about herself,
I again found myself looking for a way to explain to her who I was.
It was always difficult, for I was always anxious to get it all out — who I
was and what I did, and to explain my spirit and my life. People look at
me as just a gossip columnist, or at least that's what I thought. I told
them how much I care about my people and that I'm a storyteller. I was
pouring out as much information to them as possible, and in a hurry.*

*I told her about how I was honored to have been involved in the
reunion with Betty and Louis Farrakhan that had taken place
a few years ago. She said that that was nice and that we should
have dinner. We did so that same night. Ms. Brown is a very
wealthy retired real estate developer, and a very southern lady.
Her home was fabulous. This was Dr. Betty's favorite hangout.
When I arrived, Ms. Brown put three big, fat chicken legs, with
dressing, in the oven. She walked me through her luxurious
apartment, which had wraparound windows on the balcony.
She pointed things out: "that's Betty's Jacuzzi . . . that's Betty's
side of the bed. . . . this is the bathroom mirror where we used
to put on makeup together like young girls . . ."*

*When we sat down to dinner and she said, "Betty and I
had a lot of boyfriends," I thought, oh boy, here we go . . .*

[LAURA ROSS BROWN *is a retired real estate developer living in Alexandria, Virginia.*]

BETTY was kind of jealous where our friendship was concerned. Nobody knew Betty close-up, intimately. People only knew parts of her. There were two people who knew Betty, who knew her intimately for twenty-five years: me and Mary Redd. No matter where she was in the world, from China, from anywhere, when she got ready to come home, she would always call me from the airplane and let me know that she was arriving. For somebody to move out of your life after contact that close, move out that tragically was just too much to take. I had a call from the hospital every single morning between six and seven. I prayed for her. I'm Catholic, so I had mass said for her. I lit candles for her and I stayed on my knees.

Betty had a fabulous dinner party for me at one of the private clubs here in Washington, D.C., and invited a lot of my friends. I was updating my will and my trust at the time. We talked about that, we talked about everything. She wanted to know what I was doing with my will, and I told her. She wrote it down and did hers just like mine. I'm not giving my children all my money. I'm dividing it and giving half to my grandchildren. That's why little Malcolm ended up in her trust. She's given half to her grandchildren.

☙

WE talked about what happened after Malcolm was assassinated. I know that she was devastated. Just devastated. She didn't know where she was going or how she was going to live or what was going to happen to her. She had four little children and she was pregnant with twins, and that was, I think, one of the most devastating predicaments for a mother to find herself in. She was kind of dazed by it all, but she knew that it was going to happen and what was happening before Malcolm did. It was hard for Malcolm to believe that the Muslims were going to turn on him like they did. The other ministers living in nice houses had money, and she was not living the way she thought that they should. They didn't have money, and she would point that out to him. She was much more aware of the Muslims' hostility toward Malcolm than he was. She was smart and intuitive; she was sensitive. She knew.

We talked a little bit about Malcolm and their relationship. They had a good time. She would tell me, "Sister, your brother was fine. That was a handsome man." I said, "I know it." We talked about Malcolm and what a real man he was; you know you don't run into too many real men who really stand for something. Publicly, she did what she was supposed to do as a Muslim wife, but when she got home, she said, "a lot of that goes out the window." She talked about how they had a good, good marriage. He genuinely loved her and she genuinely loved him, even though he was gone a lot. One time she packed up and left because he was always gone and not home. He went and got her. That's what she was waiting for. She wasn't going for good — she just wanted to rattle his chain a little bit. She went home to her adoptive mother's house. Then Malcolm brought her home and he said, "The next time you leave, I'm not coming after you." She knew he meant it, and she never left again. Whatever problems they had were basically because of his time at home.

Look at what he was doing: it was like any other man working hard, building something, just like a corporate executive. He had a house-keeper for her, and she had other help and all that, but they were still not getting what all the other ministers were getting. She felt short-changed, and she was. All and all, it was a good marriage, full of love, sex, and everything. Malcolm didn't believe in cheating, so his needs were met at home with his wife.

ℬ

I met Betty in 1971 or 1972 at a Jack and Jill regional meeting in West-chester. She had the kids for the Harlem dance school there. And some of the Jack and Jill mothers didn't want those kids to dance, because the dancing seemed a little too sexy to them. I said, "Yes, let them," and why not? I had a fit. How dare they not want those kids to dance? I've always been for the underdog, and Betty was, too. I think that was our first bonding—we realized that we had that in common. And from then on, that was it. I helped her get into the Links, Inc., and I sponsored her as a trustee on the Endowment Association of the College of William and Mary, where she served for two years.

ℬ

B E T T Y worried me so. When we visited each other or traveled, we used to stay together in the same room. We could have adjoining rooms, but we'd still sleep in the same room. We'd make up our faces in the same mirror. I knew Betty's face as well as I know my own. I remember at a meeting I said, "Betty you're sick. There is something wrong with you, you don't look good. You have to stop." She'd come from China, via New York, here to a meeting in Washington. It was a thirty-hour trip, and she hadn't even changed her clothes. I said, "Betty you have got to be out of your mind." Betty was driven. And she could be funny sometimes. She said, "My other friends think I look good." I said, "Your other friends are lying. They won't tell you the truth." I mean, we were honest with one another, very honest.

And the next thing, she left here for some other occasion and went back to New York. I said, "Now, Betty, you go to bed; you're tired." She would come here and not even have packed all of her clothes. We'd go over to the White House, and here's Betty with her rubber boots on, one shoe, and a daytime purse. I had bought her four Judith Leiber purses that each cost over one thousand dollars—I said, "Now, I'm tired of seeing you with this plastic stuff, so here." So at the White House, I said, "Where is your Judith Leiber bag?" "I don't know," she said. "I left it." I said, "Here you are at the White House, and you only brought one shoe!"

When I came in the limousine to pick her up, she was never ready. I'd go tell the doorman to call Dr. Shabazz and tell her to come down because I was not coming up. She always stayed at the Mayflower. Anyway, he'd come back—"Ms. Brown, she said you'll have to come up." That meant she wasn't dressed. I had to help her get dressed.

When I got up there, she only had the one shoe, that damn plastic purse, and her rubber boots. I said, "You are running so fast that you don't even have time to pack." I said, "Now, you quit wearing that fake-fur coat." She said, "Well, you know, it's not politically correct to wear fur." I said, "I have mine on, and I dare somebody to put some paint on it. You have a fur coat, your mink. Now you hurry up and put it on." We did that kind of fussing back and forth. She said, "Sister, I'm gonna take time, I promise you, Sister." I told her to get in the bed when she went home, and not to go to work the next day, and she said, "I won't."

She was ill for a few months. I called and talked to her every day; we talked two or three times a day. At first she was really out of it, but when she got to the point where she could talk, we had some really serious conversations. She really did promise to do better, because she knew that she was killing herself. She became seriously ill. She was hospitalized for a long time and her daughter Ilyasah nursed her to health.

ℬ

BETTY copied everything I did. I was the one wearing all the St. John's knits. Betty started trying to find St. John's knits that would fit her; she would order them. Every St. John's knit I bought, Betty would try to buy it or find it somewhere. If we were going out, she'd call and ask what I was going to wear. And then Betty would show up with the same thing. I said, "Betty, we're not the gold-dust twins. You can't wear the same thing I wear."

ℬ

SOONER or later, every one of Betty's friends tried to do something about her hair. Betty liked her hair that way. I used to have trouble getting her to cut it off a little bit. Her hair was very, very thick. She had beautiful hair. Some people would ask me if she had on a wig and I'd say, "No, that's her hair." She just liked it that way, and that's the way she wore it. She pincurled her hair every night. She took good care of her skin. We'd get in the mirror, and I'd have my bag and she'd have hers. She always wanted to share. She'd say, "Now you use this on your skin and you do this and if I had something I wanted to share, I would tell her. But, basically, neither one of us used a lot; we cleaned our faces. I didn't even use foundation, but Betty did.

ℬ

H E R life was normal. She never met anybody she wanted to marry, but she certainly dated and she had long-term relationships. We dated together; I always knew who she was dating. She and I would double-date sometimes, and we always met up at the caucus weekends. A lot of times she had a date and I did too. There were a lot of men who were intimidated. Some lasted a short time because of it, one or two dates at the most.

When I got married again, Betty was very much involved. We were like Oprah Winfrey and Gayle King. She'd call in the middle of the night. No fella was going to make her lose her best friend. She called my husband "brother" and made him feel good about everything. I was widowed for about eleven years before I finally married again.

We had girl talk about fellas. She'd come here and get in my Jacuzzi and relax then put her pajamas on and we'd get in bed. We'd watch television and talk. Now, television was really funny, because Betty could not sleep without the television on. I can't sleep *with* the television on. So she'd have the television on, and pretty soon she would be snoring. Then I'd turn it off and I'd go to sleep. Next thing I know, the television's back on, and I'm awake and she's asleep — that's the way it worked.

ℬ

I T wasn't all talk, though. We did things! Betty loved to dance. We had a good time dancing in our younger days — twenty-five years ago, we had a great time. We went to clubs — we went to nightclubs and had a little cocktail here and there. We went to nightclubs and different shows of people that we liked. My favorite was Charlie Bird's, which was owned by my friends Betty Martin and her husband Bob. We went to Blues Alley, the Cellar Door—we went all over.

We traveled together. We did everything together. She came here and I went there. Over these twenty-something years, I can't remember every place we've been. We went to the Bahamas together. She wasn't always dressed up; she just didn't wear shorts. She wore pants or wrap skirts or things like that.

Once, I was working in the Bahamas, and Betty and our friend Colleen decided to visit me—we made it a vacation. So they came, she and Colleen both. Colleen came with her friend and Betty came, Betty was dating a fella in the islands then. We went to Freeport. I liked to fish, so I would get up at six o'clock every morning to go fishing with Captain Russell. I would be back at noon; by that time Colleen and Betty would be up and maybe sitting around the pool or having breakfast or sipping a glass of wine. Then we would do something in the afternoon. Colleen was not going fishing, she thought it was disgusting for somebody to get up at 6 o'clock and go fishing. And Betty was not going. So the sports stuff, I did. I swam, I went fishing. They sat and looked lovely and chatted. When I was in the pool, Betty was like, "Sister, don't you think it's time for you to go get dressed for dinner or something?" I could get in the water and stay forever; I loved to swim. Betty and Colleen stayed with me in the islands for a week or so. We were there for New Year's Eve, the Junkanoo parade, and all this kind of stuff. We went to the big New Year's Eve show. We did all kinds of fun things.

She had a very full, very normal life. Full of life and fun and dressing up with perfume and lace. Oh, and cooking. She loved fried fish, so whenever she'd come here we'd fry fish. She loved to sit out there on the balcony and eat, or sit in here and eat, but she always wanted some fried fish when she came here. I'd go buy it and fry it. She liked fish. She didn't eat pork. She loved greens. She loved soul food. It just had to be cooked with smoked turkey necks—no pork.

B

I'VE asked myself what the meaning in Betty's life was. I've asked myself that a lot. More important, I've asked myself what was the meaning of her death? What lesson was that intended to teach us? And why by her own offspring, her grandson? You know, the closest I could come to an answer for that was that Betty was passionately committed to the disadvantaged. I remember one time we were in New York, and we always got a limousine. We had a full schedule of things to do, these were all things that I had to do, and I had invited her to do them with me. She said, "I can do all of this, but Saturday at two o'clock I have to go someplace." So I planned around it. So, this Saturday, we got up, had lunch and all this, went downstairs, and got in the limousine for this two o'clock appointment. I was talking the whole time; I didn't know where we were going. It didn't really matter. We kept going, and we were going to places that looked liked a bombed out part of Lebanon or something. I said, "Betty, does the driver know where he's going?" and she said, "Oh yeah, he knows." I looked around, I couldn't imagine that we were going anywhere in this place—it looked charred up, burned up, and everything. Finally we got to this big building with a dirt yard in front and there were some people standing out there. Two or three of these people met us and took us upstairs. There was no elevator, so we walked up three floors to get to this gym. There were about twenty people there, young kids as well as some people who were sitting up on a podium. This one man who spoke, who was on the board of this community group, I think he was just really sinful in what he said—bragging about what he was doing and all, to those little disadvantaged children. That's just holding out a cookie. I thought, how could he do that? That's just unconscionable.

When Betty's turn came, she talked to them like a mother would. She told them that they could be anything they wanted to be. Don't look at where you are, she told them. Look at where you want to go. Keep focused on everything you do. Find the good in everything and praise it. She had looked at their little craft work and told them how beautiful it was, what good artists they were. They gave her a bracelet and a necklace. She made them feel so good. She put this necklace on over her St. John and she said how pretty it was. She told them, "Remember not where you are, but where you want to go in life, and focus on that." Then she said, "My friend down there, Ms. Brown, is going to write me a check for a hundred dollars"—I was always giving money for something for Betty and to Betty, too. I wrote this check for $100, and she had the little kids bring the basket around. Then she said, "All of you reporters and photographers, put some money in this basket. If you don't put any money in this basket, don't you talk to me and don't you take my picture." So there they were, everybody gave. We left the money there, and, of course, I was all part of that, I was just like Betty. I would have written a check for $500 or $1000 if she had said so and left it there with those children, because I felt that passionately about them and what they were trying to do.

What I loved the most about her was just the fact that she was Betty and she loved me so much and I loved her so much right back. It was an unconditional love that we had for each other. We always wanted the best for each other and we had fun together. We partied together, we had a good time together. We could date together; she knew that she could date together with me and nobody would ever know the who, the where, the why, or anything about it, and they never did. And there are things that I still would not say. The thing that concerned me most about Betty was the fact that she was driven and would not take care of herself. The fact that she was so, so very drained by her children; that always concerned me.

She loved her children. She wanted economic and emotional independence for her children. That was her sole purpose — she wanted each one to have a house, so much so that she bought two different apartments for the children. She was trying to get each one settled in a home. She gave Attallah money to buy her house in Los Angeles.

Betty was very much like a little girl. She was vulnerable. There was so very much she didn't know in the social skills and things, and I felt protective toward her on those things. The Links were nice to her, but she was so famous she couldn't go anywhere without security and so forth, and some were in awe of her. I guess I would say that on the whole, they were nice to her, though some were jealous. Betty could cry at the drop of a hat, and then I would have to go hug her up and make her feel better.

I remember one time I was introducing her at an event. She was going to speak, and I was saying all these nice things to introduce her. I turned around, and Betty was crying. I had to go over and hug her. Yes,

yes, yes, she could cry. Betty had a very, very hard life; it was not easy. She didn't have an easy life from birth on until she died.

Betty liked gossip. To pass on a piece of news, she would call — "Sister, did you hear anything about such and such?" She'd tease first, and then she'd go on and tell. If I heard something, I would call her. Betty had two different ways of calling me: If she called and said "Sister" in that high tone, we were going to have fun and just talk and talk. If she called at two o'clock and said "Are you asleep, wake up" in the same sentence, I knew that it was going to be a while and we were going to have to solve some world problems. I knew from the tone what we were going to talk about.

Now that we've gotten through this special tribute to "the many lives"
of Betty Shabazz, I think it's important to remember her legacy and
the legacy of her husband, El Hajj Malik El Shabazz — Malcolm X.

In the last ten years of her life, Betty became very involved with the
Little family reunions. I talked to Malcolm's second cousin, Oscar
Little, the patriarch of the family, who told me that Betty was very
well liked by Malcolm's family. At one of the reunions she showed the
family the film Malcolm X, *and she explained her position on it.*

Malcolm X was the charismatic leader of the Nation of Islam
Mosque Number Seven in New York. He was a rising star. But
while he was bringing more and more converts into the Nation,
he was also making enemies. Betty, in her speech from the New
Beginning — A Call for Justice Reunion, where she and Farrakhan
came together, said of her husband, "He spent a lot of time away
from home doing his works." It was through Malcolm that the
Nation of Islam gained their power.

Betty and Malcolm married in 1958. They were
together for seven years before he was assassinated,
and they had six children — two of whom, the twins,
were born after their father's death.

Following Malcolm's assassination, many thought that Betty would go on welfare. Instead, she returned to school to earn a master's degree and a doctorate, and then became an educator. But the Littles have a tragic history, which not even she could escape. Malcolm's grandfather died riddled with bullets; his father had his skull crushed before being laid across railroad tracks for a train to finish the job. In reaction to the murder of her husband, Malcolm's mother stopped speaking to white people — and was institutionalized for it. As a young man, Malcolm himself had been a petty thief and drug dealer who spent time in jail. While incarcerated, though, Malcolm found the Nation of Islam, became a follower of Elijah Muhammad, and transformed himself into the leader we remember today. Yet despite the example he set with his rise to prominence in the Nation, his pilgrimage to Mecca, his break with the Nation, and his tireless efforts on behalf of his people, he, too, died tragically.

Now, with Betty's death, this dark legacy haunts the family still. Qubilah, Betty and Malcolm's second child, fought substance abuse, and Betty, out of necessity, took in Qubilah's twelve-year-old son, Malcolm. Little Malcolm loved his mother, and he wanted to be with her. He did not intend to hurt his grandmother when he set the fire in the apartment; he only wanted to make her understand that he wanted to be with his mother. Betty's casket now lies with Malcolm's in the Ferncliff Cemetery in Westchester County, New York.

JEAN OWENSBY *is the president of Owensby & Co.*
Communications in New York City.

As Dr. Betty's public relations firm, we developed and coordinated events and publicity for her various Malcolm X projects. She was very picky about the projects she would allow to be named after Malcolm X. The few programs she did approve and was most proud of were the Malcom X Shabazz High School in Newark, New Jersey, and the Malcolm X Medical Scholars at Columbia University, where she graduated twenty-two doctors.

You have to remember Dr. Betty was a nurse. Ironically, she helped create the biotechnology center that is now part of the Audubon ballroom site (where her husband was slain) and that was actually growing the skin that was going to be for her other surgeries. When I asked Dr. Bruce Greenstein to speak at the memoral service he said he fell in love with Dr. Betty. He said who would think that an Orthodox Jewish doctor would fall in love with the widow of a man thought by many to be a racist, but Dr. Betty was giving him instructions with her eyes and her hands while he was working to save her life. Dr. Betty has an extraordinary spirit. That's why everyone speaks of her as she spoke of Malcolm X — in the present tense, because we know she's still here.

Dr. Betty was intensely private. She dispensed information on a need-to-know basis. But, over the years, in planning her programs and receptions, writing her press releases, invitations, and letters, and implementing her very specific instructions, we came in contact with her children, colleagues, associates, organizations, family, and friends around the world. She was truly an international citizen.

Dr. Betty was an educator and a stern taskmaster, and she demanded that you work hard, thoroughly, and quickly. In fact, we used that knowledge to plan and coordinate within seventy-two hours her memorial service at Riverside Church in New York City. It was as if Dr. Betty herself was instructing us what to do, who she wanted to speak and sing, and who she wanted to play her drum processional. We had her picture everywhere . . . there was a picture at my home on the kitchen table, which had become her planning table; there was one in my bag, in the front of my business planner; one on everyone's desk at the office; and the most important picture was placed right next to the door of the office. Early on Thursday morning, two days before her transition, when I broke down and cried, and I told everyone I couldn't complete the coordination of the memorial service, it was Dr. Betty's closest friends like Sister Aisha, Mary Redd, and Barbara Skinner who encouraged me like she would have. They told me I could do it, I *had* to do it, and I would do it.

Dr. Betty *is* hilarious. Everyone has a funny Dr. Betty story. People the world over held her in awe and she just didn't realize how many peoples' lives she touched. She paid tuitions, hospital bills, and bought diapers for strangers, for women and children who simply wrote her a letter or called her office at Medgar Evers College. She would often introduce her visitors to the school's president, Dr. Edison O. Jackson — or as she addressed him, in her proud and smiling little girl voice, "Mr. President." That's how I learned her motto "Find the good and praise it!" After introducing me to "Mr. President" one afternoon, and later while giving me a verbal dose of "don't ever give up the fight," she shared her adoptive mother's lesson with me. But her strictness and disapproval were just as palpable because some people came to her with crazy and distrustful energy. Unlike her dear friends and running buddies Myrlie Evers and Coretta Scott King, her husband's memory was often villified by people who misunderstood his great message and mission. So, she had to live her life differently—privately and more carefully than Mrs. Evers or Mrs. King.

Dr. Betty also lived for her children. She would often say, "If you want to do something for me, help my children. But, honey, let me tell you about them first!" Dr. Betty's life was motivated by helping her children throughout their lives, by continuing the powerfully positive legacy of "self-help" passed on by her boyfriend, confidant, and husband, Malcolm X.

In her efforts to further her husband's good work, Dr. Betty created her own legacy, often with "best friend" and daughter Ilyasah Shabazz at her side.

She had known me since I was five years old, and during a meeting one cold and sunny morning in her corner office at Medgar Evers College, she told me, "You grew up to be a beautiful and intelligent young woman." I know that she lived to echo those words to each of her six daughters and that those words will sustain them all. Because they were enough to keep me going for a lifetime.

It really struck me, once I got a good part of the book done, how many people had heard about it and wanted to be a part of it. Von, Eileen, and I were all getting phone calls. A lot of people who didn't know Betty personally still felt they wanted to contribute. Some just wrote a few words, as you will see here, but they are all heartfelt.

GLORIA STEINEM *is the author of* Moving Beyond Words *and a founder and now consulting editor of* Ms. *magazine, a founder of* New York *magazine and the* Ms. Foundation for Women *(a national multiracial women's fund). She travels extensively as a speaker and organizer.*

WHEN I first met Betty Shabazz, I expected a distant, private person. After all, she had not only been the partner of a great American leader but a leader who had paid the ultimate price for being public and accessible. What must it be like, I wondered, to know that such unrestrained hatred has circled your life?

I also understood that she might be suspicious of me as a white person, since whites as a group had been the original source of hatred, regardless of who pulled the trigger.

What I found was someone neither distant nor suspicious, and more gregarious than private. She was a warm, open, and accessible woman whose face seemed to be always on the verge of smiling, whether she was smiling or not. When she spoke, there was a directness and lack of pretension that signaled everyone around her to drop their pretensions. When she listened, she seemed to be absorbing the speaker as well as the words.

Only underneath, after you listened to her for a while, did you sense the bedrock of dignity, and the deep core of sadness.

We saw each other at benefits and rallies, at Harlem women's events organized by Dorothy Pitman Hughes, and during campaigns for candidates. Though we never had time to sit and talk, we did manage to discover that we had been born sixty miles apart in the Midwest (Detroit and Toledo respectively), and within two years of each other (I was the older one). We shared the experience of the conservative 1950s, Saturday afternoons going "downtown," Vernor's Ginger Ale, and a dance called the Dirty Boogie. All our time together skirted around the unspoken tragedy that had come in later years, yet it was there, a living presence.

I hoped we would sit down and talk one day. Now, that will never be. But in death as she did in life, Betty Shabazz reminds me that we cannot control what happens. It's unacceptable that she, the younger one, is not here. But as long as we remember her spirit, she will be with us.

[
WHITNEY HOUSTON *is a multi-Grammy Award–winnng singer as well as a film producer, actress, and humanitarian.*
]

WHEN Malcolm X was killed, Betty Shabazz was simply the wife of a great man. At her untimely death this past year, she was a great woman in her own right.

For every African American woman and girl child, she was the personification of strength, dignity, courage, and integrity — the daughter, the sister, the mother.

We are all more for having known her and we are all less for having lost her.

[CeCe Winans *is a Grammy Award–winning gospel singer.*]

Jesus has all wisdom. A lot of things we will never understand. He knows the end from the beginning. We all give our lives for certain reasons—you have to believe this strongly. But trust in God that He's taking them for a reason. God can give you peace. So, there are a lot of lessons to be learned from Dr. Shabazz's death. Sometimes lessons hit you in the face, but sometimes time will go by, and then, all of a sudden, you understand the lessons. It's natural to ask why Dr. Shabazz had to leave us so tragically, but it's not our part to figure out why—our part is to do what we're supposed to do and to love God first.

[Dionne Warwick *is a Grammy Award–winning singer and performer.*]

I knew Betty through her daughters, but more through all the black-movement functions we did together. Betty was always trying to teach people to get involved. She was a terrific role model. She represented strength, positiveness, and her love and regard for her folks. She expressed to me on many occasions how proud she was of me for standing tall and staying in there with our folks. Because so many of us don't.

She kept encouraging me: "You are going to get discouraged, but you can't let go."

[TIONNE ("T-BOZ") WATKINS *is part of the pop group TLC.*]

I support strong, black, independent women, like my own mother. Betty Shabazz was that kind of woman. It's really important that young black women today have role models—people they trust and look up to. It connects us to the generations of the past. Betty Shabazz was that kind of example.

[QUEEN LATIFAH *is both a television and recording star.*]

DR. Betty Shabazz will always be an inspiration to all people for her incredible courage, strength, and selflessness. She continued Malcolm's work, teaching, and lifting up those around her despite the tragedy of her husband's murder, all the while raising six children on her own. But Dr. Shabazz was never a tragic widow: She was a true Queen whose legacy stands on its own.

[BRANDY NORWOOD *appears weekly on TV's* Moesha *and is an award-winning singer and actress.*]

I admired and respected Betty Shabazz for her devotion to family and young people. To me, she was the essence of determination in spite of the odds. She was a person dedicated to making change for the good of all society.

[MARY J. BLIGE *is the queen of hip-hop soul.*]

I remember hearing about Malcolm X when I was little. My father, who was also a Muslim, had pictures of him up all over the place. I remember the one with the gun and the words "BY ANY MEANS NECESSARY." I never asked my father what that meant — I didn't know my history back then. When I learned more about the story of Malcolm's life, I understood what his purpose was. I understood why he had to go through all he went through, why he had to go to Mecca to learn how to love all colors and drink out of the same cup as a white man. My father was into all that in those days. I didn't understand why then — but now I do.

I never met Betty Shabazz, but I felt for her trauma — the way she had to lose him. I don't know why she died such a horrible death. It seems like the good people always go tragically. What a loss.

[PATTI LABELLE *is an award-winning singer*
and the author of the bestselling memoir
Don't Block the Blessings.]

I never had the opportunity to meet Dr. Betty Shabazz face to face, but I, like many others, felt as though I knew her intimately. After the death of her husband, it was inspiring to me to see how she gained strength, courage, and confidence from this tragic experience. Dr. Shabazz used the tragedy in her life to become strong. Her life became a declarative statement and a blueprint for single mothers all around the world. She became an educator, she raised six beautiful daughters who are daily reminders of their father's legacy. She became a mother figure to many, and she became an idol to me.

When I first heard of the fire that eventually took her life I was horrified. I truly believe, however, that she held on as long as she could because she knew the consequences her grandson would face if she died. Her desire to protect those she loved the most kept her holding on until she could hold on no longer. Betty had personal dignity and pride to the very end. I think that we are all better people for experiencing such a wonderful example of human spirit, dignity, and strength. I know I am.

> GLORIA NAYLOR *is the author of the bestselling novel*
> The Women of Brewster Place.

BETTY Shabazz was a very gracious and very giving woman. I spoke to her about finding a civil rights lawyer, and she was very helpful even though I had called her out of the blue. She went out of her way to recommend someone to me. She was always like that, very gracious. The first time I had any contact with Betty was during that phone conversation; I don't know if she knew who I was, but she knew I needed help. And she helped me. The reason why I went to Betty Shabazz for help is that I knew how deeply she was involved with civil rights and I knew that she would be forthcoming, based on what other people had said about her. She took my phone call immediately.

When I heard about her accident, I was horrified. Horrified that the black community had lost another pair of willing hands.

> RUBY DEE *is a television, film, and stage actress as well*
> *as an accomplished poet. The following is an excerpt from*
> *a poem she and Ossie Davis read at Dr. Betty Shabazz's*
> *funeral at the Riverside Church in New York City.*

BETTY Shabazz was dead, but now she lives. Yesterday was Harlem's day of lamentation. Great was our grief, and great our cause for grieving.

Just as Ezekiel said: "Our bones were dry, our hopes were lost, we were cut off from our parts." For Betty Shabazz—Malcolm's beloved, who when she heard the shot that tore his heart out, spread wide her arms and covered her brood like an eagle, then stood her guard where Malcolm lies forever, red fires of outrage burning in her posture—"You shall not kill my man a second time!"—that Betty—that Betty Shabazz—was dead!

That violence which 10,000 days ago took Malcolm—from which we have yet to recover—came back to claim his Betty—two devastations in a single blow. But that was yesterday.

Yesterday, death claimed his right to push his mean agenda—trampled our hope, filled another grave, and slammed the door of suffering in our face, claiming as his the prize that had no price and leaving us emptied out . . .

But that was yesterday.

Today, Betty has passed over, and so have we. From lamentation into hallelujah. Harlem is no stranger to grief: we've been to hell before, and back again. Death will not—cannot—have the final word. We have been black too long to grant him that. That honor goes to Betty. Not to death!

And there are questions here that Death cannot answer:

We ask you, Death, must partings be forever?

Are there no bonds that stretch beyond the grave?

Can we not hope that somewhere just beyond the veil of yesterday, in a world composed of children, Betty still stands, waiting to hear from us?

And this we say to her now:

Betty, God keep you safe and warm and close to Malcolm. Surely, from all this blood and fire, some solace, in your name, will take the air. From all this death, your face will rise again, singing Percy Bysshe Shelley's song of hope:

"And we will hope till hope itself creates from its own wreck the thing it contemplates."

—and are we not, from your experiences and with your help, the children of hope?

Death may take only what is his by Nature's law; the rest belongs to us, the rest is ours. Go well, Sister Betty: Your journey ends, and Malcolm steps from the shadows to greet his much beloved fresh from yesterday's deep and pain-filled river—and Malcolm will embrace you, and kiss you, and whisper in your ear. Well done, Betty. May Allah, the merciful, grant you mercy. May God, who loves all children, grant you peace.

To the family, to all who here assemble, to all the world:

Grieve if you must, but children are still dying.

Grieve, but be brief.

There's fighting to be done.

B

THOUGH many of us came to know Betty Shabazz as the wife of Malcolm X—our warrior prince—on the day of his murder, she moved from the shadows to be the guardian of his legacy and gradually to leave a legacy of her own. Throwing herself into the struggle to deflect the bullets ricocheting through the centuries, she became a warrior in her own right, touching lives as teacher, administrator, agitator, citizen. And it is to this Betty, this sister, this mother, this woman, this friend, that we speak today.

We didn't want to let you go. They said there was a 10 to 20 percent chance that you could survive. It was slim. But knowing you, Betty, your fierce determination to overcome, to raise your children, to graduate — Dr. Shabazz, to see that whatever you attended be well done — if anybody could, we knew you'd work that miracle and live. We were not prepared. We didn't want to let you go. Surely, our prayers and our blood would help see you through. Surely, your strength would do all the rest — and you would move among us again, comfort us against murder and madness.

You were so much woven into the fabric of our hope, that no matter the warnings, we were not prepared. We did not want to let you go.

What now is your agenda? What is it your death is trying to make us see about our times, our minds, our work, our love, and, above all else, our children?

How can we save them from confusion — warn them against the coming of the thingdom of greed and grossness?

How can we seed the clouds of our times with greater compassion and wisdom and love so that the waters of the coming storms will cleanse us and let us bathe the babies in virtue and joy? We did not want to let you go, but Allah called your name and you have stepped out of the marching line, making us pay attention, making us see ourselves, turning our heads toward righteousness and peace.

And so we must leave you now, dear Sister Betty, beside the still waters and the green pastures, scouting the heavens for more light to see us through.

Last Word

MAYA ANGELOU *is the winner of both the Pulitzer Prize and the National Book Award. The following is her eulogy for Dr. Betty Shabazz.*

DURING this unplanned, almost four-hundred-year sojourn, there has been much documentation describing the separation from Mother Africa. However, nothing so captures the sorrowful apartness from the mother as the venerable spiritual "Sometimes I Feel Like a Motherless Child." I speak to Betty and Malcolm's six daughters, whose parents have been wrenched from their sides in catastrophic circumstances that few are able to talk about, let alone imagine. Daughters, I want you to know that while no words can bind the broken heart, no words can heal the bruised spirits, there is some action that I hope will bring a little consolation. You need to know that there are tens of thousands, hundreds of thousands of black women who reach their arms out to you, to love you, for your mother's sake and for your sake, for your father's sake and for your sake.

These women, these black women, are powerful women inside themselves. Powerful in love who offer to enhearten you, to counsel you, to encourage you. These arms, powerful arms, which offer to protect you, to shield you, to rock you. If you turn around now and look now, you can see them here in this cathedral.

The bond of sisterhood is powerful. Indeed, I suggest that this bond has been the strongest and the most lasting bond we really have. It is through the sisterhood in the National Council of Negro Women that we have kept the mosques alive, the churches alive. It is through sisterhood —yes, it is through sisterhood—that we keep the mosques alive. It is through the National Council of Negro Women, through the Eastern Stars and Daughters of Elks that we keep our people alive. This is the truth of it.

So, when I speak of sisterhood, of course, I must speak of Betty. I can't talk much about that right now. She was my sister and I was hers, and we were strong women together. Not enough people have spoken of her humor, but Betty Shabazz was a funny woman. On top of everything else, despite the slings and arrows of an outrageous misfortune, she loved to laugh. And I never trust anybody who doesn't laugh. Those who act as if they have put airplane glue on the back of their hands and stuck them to their foreheads. Betty Shabazz could not have survived, as a wife seeing her husband murdered in front of her eyes, as a single mother, and with all that history gave her.

To become a sister to a strong woman takes incredible courage, indefinable energy, immense humor, and living love. Betty Shabazz had all of those things. So that a strong woman who is a friend says "Sister, I don't think that was the smartest thing you ever did"—it takes a strong person to say that to a strong person. On the other hand, she was the first to call if she'd seen me on television or read something of mine, to say, "Sister, you're brilliant. Girl, I love you." That takes a strong woman too, you know. There is a major seam which has come undone in the quilt of my life, major. My world, for a little while, is undone. It would have been undone totally, save that Betty Shabazz left a legacy. She's left a legacy for me and for you. In leaving little Malcolm in our hands she also means to leave him in our hearts.

> If my luck is bad
> And his aim is straight
> I will leave my life
> On the killing field.
> You can watch me die
> On the nightly news
> As you settle down
> To your evening meal.
>
> But you'll turn your back
> As you often do
> Still I am your son
> I'm your daughter too.

That man, that little man, Malcolm X's grandson, these children's son and nephew and all the grands in our inheritance. I think we must see him as we must see all the young black boys in the fell clutch of circumstance. I think we must see what we owe to those who paid for us already. Malcolm and all the young black men at risk in our bruised and beautiful past. He is our present—frightened into unspeakable terror. He is our future—bright, if we have the courage, the intelligence, the foresight to make it so. God created him, but we made him. God created him, but the society made him. And he is our inheritance.

Good-bye Betty.